MY FAVORITE OUTLINE

compiled by
CARL G. JOHNSON

BAKER BOOK HOUSE
Grand Rapids, Michigan

PHOTOLITHOPRINTED BY CUSHING - MALLOY, INC.
ANN ARBOR, MICHIGAN, UNITED STATES OF AMERICA
1977

CONTENTS

The Favorite Outline of:

Preface

Sometime ago Baker Book House published my book *My Favorite Illustration*, which contained seventy-eight illustrations of well-known speakers. In a short time the first printing was sold and it went into its second printing. When I saw that many people wanted this kind of book, the thought came to me, "Why not compile a similar one containing the favorite outlines of well-known speakers?" The publisher encouraged me to do this.

I wrote to about one hundred speakers asking them to send me their favorite sermon outline. Most of them responded, some declining, others very graciously cooperating.

I deeply appreciate and thank every speaker who shared one of their outlines so that others may profit from it, and I pray that these outlines will be blessed of God and used by many speakers as they preach ". . . the unsearchable riches of Christ" (Eph. 3:8).

My desire in gathering these sermon outlines is not to encourage laziness in preachers, but to provide a fruitful source of inspiration to those who preach. Dr. A. J. Gossip said that browsing in sermonic fields is "apt to make one rather like those larger ants who have small slaves to feed them till they have lost the power of feeding for themselves; and if you take away their slaves, although in sight of plenty, they will die." Then he continues, "If we can act like nature, taking the leaves that fall from the stately trees, and let them sink deep into the mind, and moldering there become a rich soil out of which something that is your very own springs up and flowers, then it is quite safe to read one's fellow-preachers." My prayer for every preacher of the Word is that you will take "the leaves that fall from [these] stately trees," and that through study and prayer and dependence upon the Holy Spirit, "something that is your very own springs up and flowers."

I want every one to feel free to use everything in this book to the glory of God. "Unto him be glory in the church by Christ Jesus throughout all ages, world without end. Amen" (Eph. 3:21).

Carl G. Johnson

NOW IS THE ACCEPTED TIME

II Corinthians 6:1-10

The treatment of the urgency of proclaiming the way of salvation lies in a context setting forth the motive and the manner of the Christian ministry. Chapter 5 sets forth the motives for ministry. Chapter 6:1-10 sets forth the manner of ministry. In the midst of this setting the timeliness of the message of salvation is set forth.

I. **Now is the accepted time in the dispensation of grace. World conditions indicate that time is running out.**
   A. It is the acceptable year of the Lord (Isa. 61:1-2; Luke 4:19; II Cor. 5:19; Eph. 2:8).
   B. It is to be followed by the day of vengeance of our God (Isa. 61:2).

II. **Now is the accepted time in being a season of refreshing.**
   A. It is historically true that God's "Spirit shall not always strive with men." God is "not willing that any should perish," but there are periods of revival and then of spiritual deadness.
   B. God's Spirit is working mightily now.
   C. Season of refreshing is a limited time.

III. **Now is the accepted time because the Now of the present is all we have.**
   A. There is no guarantee that tomorrow will ever come (James 4:14).
   B. There is no reason to believe that a decision will be easier to make tomorrow.

C. There is the danger of drifting past the opportune time (Heb. 2:1, 3).
   1. Danger of hardening the heart (Prov. 27:1; 29:1-2; Gal. 6:7).
   2. Danger of embracing the lie because the truth is not loved (II Thess. 2:10-11).
   3. Danger of the anticipated convenient season never coming (Acts 24:25).
D. There is the danger of character becoming fixed in its refusal of God (Gal. 6:7; Heb. 3:7-8, 15).
E. There is the danger of pleasures or ambitions absorbing the soul (e.g., the rich fool—Luke 12:19-20).
F. There is the danger of not being included in God's harvest (Jer. 8:20; cf. Heb. 9:27).
G. God "now commandeth all men everywhere to repent" (Acts 17:30).

Now is the accepted time
   It is the age of God's grace.
   It is a season of refreshing.
   It is the only time we have.
   It is the time to receive Christ for life here and hereafter.

The Favorite Outline of
WILLARD M. ALDRICH, President
Multnomah School of the Bible
Portland, Oregon

2

THE HOLY SPIRIT AND YOU

I. The Holy Spirit's work in our salvation.
A. We are convicted by the Holy Spirit (John 16:7-11).
B. We are regenerated by the Holy Spirit (John 3:5; Titus 3:5).Regeneration is an act of God the Spirit by which He instantaneously implants spiritual life in the one who receives Christ.
C. We are regenerated when we receive Jesus Christ as our personal Savior and Lord (John 1:12-13).

II. The Holy Spirit's work in our sanctification.
A. We are indwelt by the Holy Spirit (John 7:37-39; Rom. 5:5; 8:9, 11; I Cor. 6:19-20).
B. We are sealed by the Holy Spirit (II Cor. 1:22; Eph. 1:13-14; 4:30).
C. We are baptized by the Holy Spirit (I Cor. 12:13).
D. We are commanded to be filled with the Holy Spirit (Eph. 5:18).
E. We are commanded to walk in the Holy Spirit (Gal. 5:16).

III. The Holy Spirit's work in our service.
A. We are empowered by the Holy Spirit (Acts 1:8).
B. We are called into God's service by the Holy Spirit (Acts 13:4).
C. We are led by the Holy Spirit (Acts 8:26, 29; Rom. 8:14).

The Favorite Outline of
HYMAN J. APPELMAN, Evangelist
Kansas City, Missouri

3

GENUINE CHRISTIANITY AND MODERN ATTITUDES TOWARD IT

I Corinthians 1:23-24

Christianity has today become a fallen term. For many it has lost its original meaning and has become a "Mother Hubbard" expression covering both truth and error. Under the umbrella of the name are ever increasing, widely differing cults, creeds, and programs. These may range from cold liberalism to fiery fanaticism; loose worldliness to hidebound Pharisaism; Christ without a cross to a cross without a Christ.

To the apostles and early Christians, Christianity was not primarily a creed or competitive cult but a marvelous story. It was good news to a lost world—a crucified Son of God who bore our sins in His body on the cross, bringing forgiveness of sin and life eternal to those who had faith in Him.

Christ Crucified—the Lamb slain, risen, and coming again—transformed millions.

I. Genuine Christianity is an established fact.
    A. A historical fact. That Christ lived, died, rose, and ascended is as historical as that Abraham Lincoln lived and was assassinated.
        1. Not cheap sentiment culled from exciting or charismatic excesses.
        2. Not an immunity bath in salvation's fountain.
        3. Not the gushy, insipid "Luv" syndrome.

4. A fact of history. God in the person of His Son inserted Himself into human history and experience, and at a definite place and time died for mankind's sin.
B. A theological fact.
1. Theology is the science of God. The theology of the cross:
   a. reveals the divine plan for human redemption—Christ died a substitute for sinners.
   b. reveals the meaning of Old Testament symbols and sacrifices.
   c. reveals the prophesied Messiah, despised and rejected.
   d. is the basis of God's righteousness and man's peace.
2. Living faith in the crucified Christ is the sole lever that lifts the individual and society out of the pit of moral degradation into which we have fallen.
3. Christ crucified is the power of God unto salvation (Rom. 1:16).

II. Paul says there are three attitudes toward genuine Christianity.

A. Attitude of the Jews: formalism, ritualism, "stumbling block."
1. That the Messiah should die upon the cross is unthinkable! "A rock of offence" (Isa. 8:14; Rom. 9:33).
2. Jewish religion represents ritual religion, beautiful symbolism.
3. "Stumbling block" (Greek *scandalon*—"scandal"). Christ crucified for sin is still a scandal to ritualism.
B. Attitude of the Greeks: intellectualism.
1. "Foolishness" (Greek *Morian*—"moron").

2. A crucified Christ is not philosophical enough for cultured Greeks.
3. Today, modern education and theology reject the cross, the sacrifice of innocent for guilty. Abhorrent! The blood of the cross is despised by modern learning.

C. Attitude of the believer: God's wisdom, power ("dynamite").
1. Man's wisdom is foolishness by comparison.
"I will destroy the wisdom of the wise, and bring to nothing the understanding of the foolish" (I Cor. 1:19).
2. The so-called great religious thinkers are flabbergasted (stand aghast) at God's redemptive wisdom.
Live through One that *died;*
Blessed through One who was made a *curse;*
Justified through One who was *condemned.*
3. Christ crucified:
a. vindicates the righteousness of God,
b. pays the penalty for sin,
c. maintains man's moral freedom.

Small wonder that Isaac Watts should say:
When I survey the wondrous cross . . .
I pour contempt on all my pride.
or Cowper:
Dear dying Lamb, Thy precious blood
Shall never lose its power.
or Bennard:
So I'll cherish the old rugged cross . . .
And exchange it some day for a crown.

The Favorite Outline of
WILLIAM WARD AYER,
Executive Director
Ayerow Christian Projects, Inc.
St. Petersburg, Florida

THE GREATEST, GRAVEST QUESTION
THAT YOU WILL EVER ANSWER

Questions aplenty are found penned on the pages of Scripture. But, doubtless, the greatest, gravest question that was ever asked and had to be answered was the question of the weak-willed, spineless governor Pilate in a cowardly attempt to save his political position, salve his conscience, and satisfy a honed-on-hatred crowd as he cried out in desperation, "What shall I do then with Jesus which is called Christ?" (Matt. 27:22).

I. **This question must be answered by everyone of us individually because:**
   A. We are born by individual births.
   B. We live individual lives.
   C. We die individual deaths (II Sam. 14:14; Rom. 5:12; Heb. 9:27; James 1:14-15).
   D. We face God the Judge individually (Rom. 14:11-12; Rev. 20:11-15).
   E. We will spend eternity somewhere individually.

II. **This question must be answered by everyone of us specifically.** "What shall I *do* then with Jesus?"
   A. You must *love* Him or *hate* Him (Matt. 6:24).
   B. You must be *for* Him or be *against* Him (Matt. 12:30).
   C. You must *confess* Him or *deny* Him (Matt. 10:32-33).
   D. You must *crown* Him Lord or *crucify* Him (Rom. 10:13; Heb. 6:4-6).
   E. You must *receive* Him or *reject* Him (John 1:11-12).

7

All these decisions must be made specifically about Jesus who is the Christ:

He is the only way to heaven (John 14:6); He has the only name that counts in heaven (Acts 4:12); He is the only mediator (I Tim. 2:5-6); and He gave His blood as the only remedy for sin (I John 1:7).

III. Your answer to this question determines your destiny forever.

A. Pilate chose to reject Christ instead of release Him, and that decision led to his political defeat and his eternal doom.

B. *Today* you must decide: "What will I do then with Jesus?" It is your choice and it will determine your life, your death, your eternity.

> It's your life—and you can abuse it.
> It's your soul—and you can lose it.
> It's Heaven or Hell—as you choose it—
> But remember—it's God's love that you
>   are throwing away!

The Favorite Outline of
FRED M. BARLOW,
Sunday School Consultant
Regular Baptist Press
Lakeland, Florida

SEVEN WAYS TO BE JUSTIFIED

Job 9:2

Justification means more than being pardoned or forgiven. When the believer is justified he is vastly more than a forgiven criminal. Justification is that act which originates in the heart of God, and which removes guilt with its liabilities and pronounces the believing sinner blameless.

The Scriptures reveal seven ways by which an individual may be justified, and as we face these truths we shall find the inspired answer to Job's question in our text above.

I. We are justified by God.

The Bible declares, "It is God that justifieth" (Rom. 8:33). The Word is very clear and leaves no one in doubt as to the source of justification. When He justifies, He gives to the believing sinner a perfect standing, a position equal to His own, and a righteousness that is the equivalent to Christ's.

II. We are justified by grace.

The Scriptures say, "Being justified freely by his grace through the redemption that is in Christ Jesus" (Rom. 3:24), and "that being justified by his grace, we should be made heirs according to the hope of eternal life" (Titus 3:7).

III. We are justified by blood.

"Much more then, being now justified by his blood, we shall be saved from wrath through him" (Rom. 5:9).

9

This passage states the price which was paid in order to make possible this wonderful and glorious act of justification.

IV. We are justified by resurrection.
Paul wrote, ". . . who was delivered for our offences, and was raised again for our justification" (Rom. 4:25). The resurrection of our Savior from the grave is the proof that His work on the cross was fully accomplished and was satisfactory to God. The Living One is the assurance to the condemned one that there is no condemnation.

V. We are justified by life.
"Therefore as by the offence of one judgment came upon all men to condemnation; even so by the righteousness of one the free gift came upon all men unto justification of life" (Rom. 5:18). As the believer was in union with the death of Christ and thus died to the old life, so is he in union with the risen life of Christ, and being in such a life, he is justified. Since we are in the risen Christ, we are accepted in Him before God.

VI. We are justified by faith.
"Therefore being justified by faith, we have peace with God through our Lord Jesus Christ" (Rom. 5:1). Again we read, "And by him all that believe are justified from all things . . ." (Acts 13:39). Faith is the means by which we avail ourselves of what God is offering by way of justification. Faith is not the justification, but the method by which justification is accepted.

VII. We are justified by works.
We read in James, "Ye see then how that by works a man is justified, and not by faith only" (2:24). This apostle is not at variance with Paul who wrote, "But to him that worketh not, but believeth on him that justifieth the ungodly, his faith is counted for

10

righteousness" (Rom. 4:5). Paul is speaking from the divine viewpoint. When James speaks of being justified by works he is presenting the issue from man's viewpoint. Men cannot see faith like God can; they can see it only as evidenced by what is done. Hence, before men our works are the evidence of the justification which is ours through faith in the Lord Jesus Christ.

The Favorite Outline of
R. S. BEAL, Pastor Emeritus
First Baptist Church
Tucson, Arizona

WHEN I SEE THE BLOOD

Exodus 10:28-29; 11:4–12:13; Text 12:12-13

I. Retribution.
A. Judgment fell on Egypt, the land of bondage.
B. God's curse hangs over the world (Ps. 7:11; John. 3:36; Gal. 1:4).

II. Substitution.
A. A lamb was slain for each family (John. 1:29; I Cor. 5:7; I Peter 1:18-19).
B. The lamb had to be without spot or blemish (Exod. 12:3-6; Heb. 4:15).
C. The lamb's blood had to be shed (Lev. 17:11; Matt. 27:25; Heb. 9:22).
D. The lamb's body had to be roasted with fire.

III. Appropriation.
A. The deliverance of the passover lamb had to be appropriated (Exod. 12:3-5; Ps. 51:7; Isa 55:6; Rom. 10:17; I John 1:7).
B. Those who did not appropriate the blood suffered the judgment of God.

When all mankind is judged by God, only those people who have appropriated the protection of the blood will be safe.

The Favorite Outline of
THOMAS E. BERRY, Pastor
Baptist Bible Church
Elkton, Maryland

THE GREATEST MESSAGE IN THE WORLD

John 3:16

In the text is found great, profound spiritual truths that relate to salvation. Though it be just a small verse, just a few words, yet God has revealed to us His entire plan of salvation in this one verse.

I. The author of salvation: "God."

This is the God who made the universe. This is the God who made all that is in the world in which we live. This is the author of the salvation that I'm talking about.

II. The affection of salvation: "so loved the world."

In spite of all our sins, in spite of all we have done wrong, in spite of everything contrary to the will of God, God so loved the world! It includes all the nations of the world. It includes all the islands in the sea. It includes all the black and white, rich and poor, educated and uneducated, young and old—everyone.

III. The agony of salvation: "that he gave."

In the salvation that God provided for you and me there was wrapped up the agony of the heart of God Himself and the agony of the physical and spiritual sufferings of Jesus Christ in the few hours before He died. Oh, the agony of salvation!

IV. The advocate of salvation: "his only begotten Son."

Jesus became our advocate by dying upon the cross that our sins might be forgiven. An advocate is one who pleads another's cause. Thank God, an advocate was provided for us to plead our cause before God.

V. The availability of salvation: "that whosoever."
This salvation is for "whosoever," and that includes you, me, everybody you know, and everybody you don't know.

VI. The acceptance of salvation: "believeth in him."
The word *believeth* means that a person has to receive Christ, trust Him, and put his faith in Him to be saved. (See John 1:12; 5:24; 20:31; Acts 16:31; Eph. 2:8-9.)

VII. The alternative to salvation: "should not perish."
There is an alternative to this salvation: without it a person will perish—be lost forever. If you refuse to receive Jesus Christ as your personal Savior and Lord there is no alternative but to perish forever. Never any ending to your punishment; never any cessation of torment; never any ending of your separation from God! Jesus spoke much about hell (Matt. 5:22, 29-30; 10:28; 11:23; 16:18; 18:9; 23:15, 33; Mark 9:43, 45, 47; Luke 10:15; 12:5; 16:23).

VIII. The abiding salvation: "but have everlasting life."
Oh, how I thank God that the Bible promises everlasting life to those who put their trust in Jesus Christ, and that it starts the very moment Christ is received. In the New Testament the kind of life God gives to those who receive His Son is called "eternal" or "everlasting" forty-four times. (See John 3:15-16, 36; 5:24; 6:40; 10:28; 17:2-3; Rom. 6:23; I John 5:11, 13.)

Oh, my friend, do you have it tonight? Have you received Jesus Christ as your personal Savior? If not, do so right now.

The Favorite Outline of
JOHN L. BRAY, Evangelist
Plant City, Florida

14

BUILDING A SUCCESSFUL CHRISTIAN LIFE

I Corinthians 3:9-17

"We are labourers together with God" (v. 9). God gives us the marvelous opportunity of having a piece of the action in the success of our lives as we produce a work that is coordinated with His. Note also that the apostle Paul states his ambition to be a "wise master-builder," a *sophos architekton,* a sophisticated architect in building both his own personal life and also enabling the lives of others and the life of the church to be built.

We have four principles that are significant in building a successful Christian life.

I. Begin with an adequate foundation.
"For other foundation can no man lay than that which is laid, which is Jesus Christ" (v. 11). Foolish people choose the foundation of human wisdom, personal riches, worldly acclaim. Here we have the assertion that the only foundation is Christ. Justification by faith is the beginning of the Christian life.

II. Proceed according to the proper plan.
"But let every man take heed how he buildeth upon it" (v. 10). The adequate, spacious, strong foundation of Jesus Christ implies a building that is commensurate with that foundation. The foundation is the work of Christ alone, but we are to "take heed," for the building upon that foundation is the sense in which we are workers together with God.

III. Use adequate construction materials.
"Now if any man build upon this foundation gold, silver, precious stones, wood, hay, stubble . . ." (v. 12).

The construction material list given here is divided into two classes:
A. Expensive, incombustible: gold, silver, precious stones.
B. Cheap, combustible: wood, hay, stubble.

IV. Build against the testing time.
"Every man's work shall be made manifest: for the day shall declare it" (v. 13a). There is a test, a judgment, to come for each of us, and that judgment certainly arrives in two ways:
A. In this life, testings that are common to man will press upon us.
B. In the life to come, we must all appear before the judgment seat of Christ (II Cor. 5:10).

How wonderful to contemplate the rewards that shall follow as we have built successfully for Christ in this world.

The Favorite Outline of
DAVE BREESE, President
Christian Destiny, Inc.
Wheaton, Illinois

THE MISTAKE OF A LIFETIME

Luke 12:16-34

This is the story of the rich fool.

I. He was successful.
   A. Physically.
   B. Materially.
   C. Socially.

II. He was sincere.
   A. He thought within himself.
   B. Sincerity is good, but not enough for salvation.

III. He was self-centered.
   A. He thought only of himself.
   B. Notice the prominence of the word *I* and the personal pronouns in the story.

IV. He was short-sighted.
   A. He thought only of the present and the immediate.
   B. He gave no thought for the future.
   C. He sacrificed the future on the altar of the immediate.

V. He was stripped of everything.
   A. Just when he thought he was ready to live he had to die.
   B. To gain the whole world and lose your soul is a bad bargain (Mark 8:36).

VI. He was a striking example (in a negative way).
   A. Don't plan just for the present.

17

B. Don't provide just for the flesh.
C. Make provision for your soul's eternal destiny.

Trust Christ as your personal Savior and be saved (Acts 16:31).

The Favorite Outline of
HOMER BRITTON, Evangelist
Chattanooga, Tennessee

THE FIVE HORSEMEN IN THE BOOK OF REVELATION

Revelation 6:1-8; 19:11-16

The outline for the Book of Revelation is found in Revelation 1:19. God gave John a threefold outline for the book. In Revelation 1 we have the things of the past tense, the vision that John had of Jesus Christ. In Revelation 2 and 3 we have the things of the present tense, the Church Age. From Revelation 4 through the end of the book we have the things of the future tense. After Revelation 4, the word *church* is not used again until the last chapter. While all the judgments of God are taking place here on earth, the Church is with its Savior, the Lord Jesus Christ. When the things spoken of in this message take place, the saved will have been raptured.

I. **Deceiver, or Antichrist (Rev. 6:1-2).**
   The word *antichrist* is used only four times, and that by John in I John 2:18, 22; 4:3; II John 7. Note three things about the deceiver:
   A. The moment of his appearance (II Thess. 2:6-8): when the Holy Spirit is taken out of the world in His restraining power; that is, the rapture.
   B. The manner of his appearance (II Thess. 2:9).
   C. The message of his appearance (II Thess. 2:4).

II. **Destroyer (Rev. 6:3-4).**
   A. Purpose: "To take peace from the earth." Ezekiel says, "Every man's sword shall be against his brother . . ." (38:21). There will not be a spot on the face of the globe where there is not war.

There will be race wars, class wars, and religious wars. In the Old Testament a time similar to this is mentioned in II Chronicles 15:3, and the result of that time was found in II Chronicles 15:5-6. There was no peace anywhere.

B. Program: "There was given unto him a great sword" (Rev. 6:4). The word *sword* means "something that can be concealed, that has the power of life and death." His program will be bloodshed, indicating a terrible battle. It will take seven months to bury the dead bodies, seven years to clean up the debris from the battle.

III. Dearth (Rev. 6:5-6).

Three problems confront the world today. The first two bring about the third.

A. Inflation. This rider sells a measure of wheat for a penny. In Christ's day, a man would earn a penny for a day's work. He could buy eight measures of wheat for a penny. But in the tribulation, a man will only be able to buy one measure of wheat. That means that prices will rise eight times higher than normal. Men will not be able to buy or sell unless they have been stamped by the Antichrist. James 5:1-3 shows the folly of storing up riches.

B. Overpopulation. It is predicted now that every thirty-five years the population will double. In Jesus' day there were 200 million people; in 1650, 500 million; in 1850, 1 billion; in 1930, 2 billion; and today, about 4 billion.

C. Famine. He sells three measures of barley for a penny. Because men will not be able to live on a slave's subsistence, they will turn to the food of livestock—barley (see Lam. 4:9; 5:10).

IV. Death (Rev. 6:7-8).

"Behold a pale horse" (the color of a corpse or leprous skin).

A. Companion: "Hell" follows. Hell will have to enlarge itself to make room for everyone who will be cast there (Isa. 5:14).

B. Conquest: "One fourth of the earth." In World War I there were 8 million casualties; in World War II, 78 million. All wars combined have produced about 150 million casualties. This rider would wipe out over 800 million.

V. Deliverer (Rev. 19:11-16).

He is called "Faithful and True, . . . The Word of God, . . . KING OF KINGS, AND LORD OF LORDS."

A. His wardrobe (v. 13; see also Isa. 63:2-4).

B. His witnesses (v. 14). These are the children of God (John 14:3; Col. 3:4; II Thess. 1:7-10).

C. His weapon (v. 15; see also Isa. 11:4).

The Bible says that one day every knee shall bow (Phil. 2:9-11). One day Judas, Mussolini, Stalin, and Lenin will bend their knees and confess that Jesus is Lord. You will too. Do it today because you want to, don't wait until then and bow because you have to.

The Favorite Outline of
RON COMFORT, Evangelist
Clarksburg, West Virginia

SEVEN SIGNS OF SONSHIP

John 3:7-8

The Christian life begins with a birth. The new life doesn't begin with a baptism, a sprinkling, a completion of a course of studies on the doctrines of the church; the Christian life begins with a spiritual birth.

Physical life begins with a birth. "That which is born of the flesh is flesh . . ." (John 3:6a). That which is born of the flesh will always bring forth "after its kind," or the natural life—the fruit of the natural, carnal, fleshly being. Thus, a "new birth" is essential to being a Christian. One birth is not sufficient. There must be the second birth, the new birth, the spiritual birth, which is a birth from above.

John 3 deals with the subject of the "new birth," and several signs of sonship as a result of the new birth are given in this chapter. Take a long, hard, honest look at your life to see if these signs are evident.

I. A person who is spiritual.

The first sign evidenced after being born again is that the person becomes a "spiritual being," when heretofore he was only a carnal, fleshly being. Are you a spiritual person? Are you seeking God's will for your life, and studying His Word? Do you pray? Have you been changed by the new birth? "So is every one that is born of the Spirit" (v. 8).

22

II. A person of faith.

The second sign of sonship is that children of God evidence a life of faith. John 3:16 has been called "the Bible in a nutshell." This verse contains the fact of God, His love and His great love gift, and this verse contains the simple way of salvation—"whosoever *believeth*." Believing faith is a sign of spiritual sonship. Walking by faith is the sign of a growing Christian, who not only trusts Christ to save his soul, but has learned to trust for "daily bread."

III. A person of no condemnation.

The third spiritual sign of sonship evidenced after the new birth is that the child of God does not live and labor under a guilt complex or condemnation (John 3:18). The major problem is sin, and when that is settled, a Christian can walk without condemnation and go to sleep at night "safe in the arms of Jesus."

IV. A person who "doeth righteousness."

The fourth spiritual sign of sonship is noted in John 3:21: "But he that doeth truth cometh to the light, that his deeds may be made manifest, that they are wrought in God." A saved person "doeth truth," or "doeth righteousness." His deeds are "wrought in God." In plain and simple language, a born-again child of God doesn't walk in the ways of the world and of sin, but he lives like a Christian.

V. A person who is obedient.

The fifth sign of sonship is obedience. In John 3:22, baptism is mentioned, which in Matthew 29:19 (the Great Commission) is commanded by Jesus, along with teaching, to be obeyed. The willingness to teach or be taught and to baptize or be baptized characterizes a Christian's obedience to the Lord.

VI. A person who witnesses.

It is reported that John the Baptist witnessed for

Jesus (v. 26). It would seem to be natural for a person to talk about Christ. Being born of the Spirit, and thereby a child of God, it would seem to be almost automatic.

But, most people are not witnessing for Christ. *Yet one of the greatest signs of sonship is witnessing because we love Him!* Have you told anyone about Jesus today?

VII. A person who glorifies Christ.

The seventh sign of spiritual sonship is summed up in the words of John the Baptist in John 3:30, "He must increase, but I must decrease." John was saying, "I must glorify Christ in all that I do. He must have the glory. He must be exalted. He must increase. I must decrease and stay in the background!"

Well, how do you "measure up"? Are these signs evidenced in your life today? Have you "checked up" on yourself? Happy are you if these seven signs are real in your heart and life.

If not, perhaps you are cold and backslidden and need to repent and return to Christ. Or perhaps these signs are not evidenced in your life because you have not been born of the Spirit of God!

If you are not saved, then today I plead with you, repent of sin, believe from the depths of your heart on the Lord Jesus Christ as personal Savior, and *be saved today!*

The Favorite Outline of
BRUCE D. CUMMONS, Pastor
Massillon Baptist Temple
Massillon, Ohio

THE HIGH COST OF BEING LOST

Have you thought about what it costs if you're not saved at all? What it costs if you're not a Christian? What it costs if you don't believe in Jesus?

I. **It will cost you the greatest peace on earth.**
   A. People with Christ have real peace (John 14:27).
      1. Peace with God (Rom. 5:1).
      2. Peace of God (Isa. 26:3; Phil. 4:6-7).
   B. People without Christ have no peace (Isa. 57:20-21; Rom. 3:17).

II. **It will cost you the greatest possession on earth.**
   A. Your greatest possession is your soul (Mark 8:36).
   B. It would be a terrible bargain to gain the world and lose your soul (Mark 9:43-48).

III. **It will cost you the greatest partnership on earth.**
   A. You can have the partnership of Jesus Christ in your life (Matt. 28:20).
   B. You will have the partnership of the devil in your life if Jesus Christ is not your personal Savior (John 8:44).

IV. **It will cost you the greatest penalty on earth.**
   A. If you have Jesus Christ as your personal Savior you are saved from the penalty of sin, which is hell (Rom. 5:8-9).
   B. If you do not have Jesus Christ as your personal Savior you will have to pay the penalty of sin, and go to hell forever (Rom. 6:23a; Rev. 21:8).

Won't you let Him save you now? "Believe on the Lord Jesus Christ, and thou shalt be saved" (Acts 16:31).

The Favorite Outline of
E. J. DANIELS, Director
Christ for the World
Orlando, Florida

THE POWER OF THE BLOOD

Leviticus 17:11; Matthew 26:28

In considering this great Bible doctrine there are two things I would like to establish immediately.

1. The importance of the blood of Christ in the plan of redemption (Heb. 9:22).
2. The invitation to all men to be forgiven and redeemed (Matt 20:28; I Tim. 2:6).

There are several things I wish to point out in our study on the power of the blood.

I. It is perfect in its analysis.

". . . I have betrayed the innocent blood" (Matt. 27:4; see also John 8:46; 18:38; Heb. 7:26; 12:24; I Peter 2:22; I John 3:5).

II. It is purifying in its application.

"How much more shall the blood of Christ . . . purge your conscience from dead works . . ." (Heb. 9:14; see also Isa. 53:10).

III. It is perpetual in its action.

"But if we walk in the light, as he is in the light, we have fellowship one with another, and the blood of Jesus Christ his Son cleanseth us from all sin" (I John 1:7; see also Ps. 119:5; John 3:19-21; 8:12).

IV. It is powerful in its accomplishments.

". . . unto him that loved us, and washed us from our

sins in his own blood" (Rev. 1:5b; see also John 8:36; Eph. 1:7; Heb. 2:15).

V. It is permanent in its acquittal.
". . . by his own blood he entered in once into the holy place, having obtained eternal redemption for us" (Heb. 9:12; see also 9:26; 10:12).

VI. It is protective in its appropriation.
"Wherefore Jesus also, that he might sanctify the people with his own blood, suffered without the gate" (Heb. 13:12; see also Exod. 11:7; 12:13).

VII. It is precious in its appraisal.
". . . ye were not redeemed with corruptible things, as silver and gold, from your vain conversation received by tradition from your fathers; but with the precious blood of Christ, as of a lamb without blemish and without spot" (I Peter 1:18-19; see also 2:7).

VIII. It is peace-assuring in its affirmation.
"And, having made peace through the blood of his cross, by him to reconcile all things unto himself . . ." (Col. 1:20).

IX. It is profuse in its appeal.
"If we confess our sins, he is faithful and just to forgive us our sins, and to cleanse us from all unrighteousness" (I John 1:9).

The Favorite Outline of
ALLEN P. DICKERSON, Pastor
Maranatha Baptist Church
Elkton, Maryland

THE PLAIN MAN'S PATHWAY TO HEAVEN

Romans 10:13

This verse, no doubt, has been used by the Spirit of God to bring more people to Jesus Christ than any other verse in the Bible. So important are these words that God has given them to us three times. Not only do we find them here in Romans 10:13, but also in Joel 2:32 and Acts 2:21.

Surely the key word in explaining the effectiveness of this verse is *simplicity*. In fact, one of the chief goals of Satan is to corrupt and complicate the gospel (II Cor. 11:3). Now let us consider in detail this simple yet glorious salvation.

I. God's proclamation: "shall be saved."

A. Salvation is definite—it is possible to be saved!

B. Salvation defined—to be saved is to be delivered (Joel 2:32).

C. Salvation detailed.

1. It involves eternity.

   a. We are in danger as sinners of losing our souls in hell.

   b. God has said that He will deliver us from eternal destruction to eternal life.

2. It includes this life.

   a. God desires not only to deliver our souls, but our lives as well.

   b. We are bent on self-destruction.

II. God's proposition: "shall call upon the name of the Lord."

A. The "center" of this verse is:
   1. not our name,
   2. not our family's name,
   3. not our church's name, but
   4. the name which is above every name (Matt. 1:21; Acts 4:12; Phil. 2:9-11). (A name is *who* a person is and *what* he has done.)

B. The "call" of this verse is a:
   1. call for help—repentance;
   2. call from the heart—not mere words;
   3. call of hope—faith.

III. God's perimeter: "whosoever."

A. The rich and the poor.
B. The educated and the uneducated.
C. The church member and the nonchurch member.
D. The young and the old.

No wonder the writer of Hebrews declares it "so great salvation." It is great in its *purpose*, great in its *plan*, and most of all, great in the *Person* who made salvation possible for us.

The Favorite Outline of
PAUL DIXON, Evangelist
Cedarville, Ohio

HEAVEN, MY FUTURE HOME

John 14:1-3; Hebrews 11:8-10

I. Heaven is a prepared place for a prepared people (John 14:1-6).

II. Heaven has been the hope of believers in all ages.
   A. Abraham was looking for a city (Heb. 11:10).
   B. Moses refused to be called the son of Pharaoh's daughter (Heb. 11:24-26).
   C. Paul said, "We have a building of God . . . eternal in the heavens" (II Cor. 5:1).
   D. The martyrs longed to go there (Heb. 11:35).

III. Heaven will be a place of indescribable beauty (Rev. 21–22).

IV. Heaven will be a place of perfect health (Rev. 21:4).

V. Heaven will be a place where sin cannot enter (Rev. 21:27).

VI. Heaven will be a place of perfect knowledge (I Cor. 13:12).

VII. Heaven will be a place of eternal reunion.
   A. With Christ (Rev. 21:3).
   B. With loved ones (I Thess. 4:17).

Jesus is the way to heaven (John 14:6).
God has provided an all-sufficient salvation.
　　　　It is perfect in its nature.
　　　　It is universal in its extent.
　　　　It is free in its communication.

It is eternal in its duration.

It is present in its application.

Will you receive God's salvation and meet me in heaven? I pray you will.

> *The Favorite Outline of*
> W. E. DOWELL, President
> Baptist Bible College
> Springfield, Missouri

THE HOLY SPIRIT

I. Know Him (John 14:16-18).
A. As a real person (John 16:13-15).
B. As living within (I Cor. 6:19).
C. As a constant companion (Rom. 8:14).

How can we know him? The answer is in Ephesians 1:17-20. We need divine revelation in God's Word of a Bible fact by the Holy Spirit concerning Himself.

II. Obey Him (Acts 5:32).
A. Listen to Him (in the Word, in your heart).
B. Immediately in everything.
C. Don't grieve Him (Eph. 4:30).

III. Yield to Him (Rom. 8:8-13).
A. Surrender your will (ambition, recognition, desires).
B. Surrender your all (Rom. 6:13; 12:1).
   1. Body.
   2. Mind.
   3. Heart.
   4. Life.

The Favorite Outline of
DARRELL DUNN, Evangelist
Chattanooga, Tennessee

THE FIVE LOOKS OF SCRIPTURE

I. We are condemned by a look.
"And when the woman saw that the tree was good for food, and that it was pleasant to the eyes, and a tree to be desired to make one wise, she took of the fruit thereof, and did eat, and gave also unto her husband with her; and he did eat. And the eyes of them both were opened, and they knew that they were naked" (Gen. 3:6-7a).

II. We are converted by a look.
"Look unto me, and be ye saved, all the ends of the earth: for I am God, and there is none else" (Isa. 45:22).

"And Moses made a serpent of brass, and put it upon a pole, and it came to pass, that if a serpent had bitten any man, when he beheld the serpent of brass, he lived" (Num. 21:9; see also John 3:14-15).

III. We are challenged by a look.
"Looking unto Jesus the author and finisher of our faith; who for the joy that was set before him endured the cross, despising the shame, and is set down at the right hand of the throne of God" (Heb. 12:2).

IV. We will be caught up by a look.
"Looking for that blessed hope, and the glorious appearing of the great God and our Saviour Jesus Christ" (Titus 2:13).

V. We will be captivated by a look.

"And they shall see his face; and his name shall be in their foreheads" (Rev. 22:4).

The Favorite Outline of
DAVID OTIS FULLER, Former Pastor
Wealthy Street Baptist Church
Grand Rapids, Michigan

PAUL'S FOUR AMBITIONS

Philippians 3:10-11

Ambitious people try to accomplish worthwhile things.
Ambition is spurred by vision (Prov. 29:18):
> a vision of God to fear Him, serve Him (Isa. 6:1-8);
> a vision of hell—shun it; of heaven—gain it;
> a vision of a lost world—win it (Matt. 9:35-38).

I. "That I may know him."
A. Paul met Jesus about thirty years before (Acts 9:1-6).
B. To know Him is to love Him, and ever desire to know more about Him.
C. We know people by communication and fellowship, by living with them. To know God:
1. Read the Bible (Ps. 119:9, 11).
2. Commune with Him (Rev. 3:20).

II. "The power of his resurrection."
A. Paul is not speaking of the resurrection of the dead.
B. Paul had hate and murder in his heart before seeing Jesus. The Holy Spirit put within Paul a new heart, a new desire, and a new purpose for living (II Cor. 5:17).
C. Paul wanted the Holy Spirit to keep this great power upon him.

III. "The fellowship of his sufferings."
A. Paul did not mind suffering for Jesus.
B. Do we? In the home, on the job, in school, on all occasions? What about pleasure? T.V.? Selfish ambitions?

IV. "I might attain unto the resurrection of the dead."

A. Two resurrections:
1. First resurrection for Christians (I Cor. 15:51-52; I Thess. 4:13-18).
2. Second resurrection (Rev. 20:11-15).

B. There is a blessed hope for the Christian (Phil. 3:20-21; Titus 2:11-14; I John 3:2-3).

The Favorite Outline of
BYRAM H. GLAZE, President
Calvary Crusade, Inc.
Columbus, Georgia

THE ISSUES FROM DEATH

Psalm 68:20

"He that is our God is the God of salvation; and unto God the Lord belong the issues of death."

I. The design of death.

A. Diabolical (Heb. 2:14).

The ultimate tool of Satan is death. Praise God for victory through Christ Jesus.

B. Deceptive (James 1:13-15).

Even though the wages of sin is death, the devil is very subtle in his approach. No man ever thinks consciously of death when he sins.

C. Degrading (Rom. 5:12-21).

The course of death is ever downward. Sin never elevates.

II. The devastation of death.

A. Depriving (Gen. 3:23-24).

Because of sin, Adam and Eve lost their heritage from the Lord and were driven out of the Garden of Eden. Sin also takes our loved ones from us through the route of death.

B. Defiling (John 11).

No matter how much we love our relatives, death is defiling and we must bury their bodies as soon as possible.

C. Demanding (Phil. 2:5-8; Heb. 12:2).

Only the death of the only begotten Son of God could avail anything for us in the conflict against death. It cost God heaven's best to give us victory over our last enemy.

III. The defeat of death.
A. Divine (John 11:22-27; I Cor. 15:21-26).
   Triumph over our last enemy was accomplished through the miraculous bodily resurrection of Jesus Christ from the dead.
B. Dramatic (Matt. 28:1-9).
   So incongruous was the presence of eternal life in the presence of death that life's greatest drama was portrayed by Jesus arising from the dead.
C. Delightful (I Cor. 15:51-58).
   Not only do we overcome death through life by Jesus Christ, but we also anticipate the Rapture which will enable one generation of Christians to cheat death completely. Praise the Lord!

The Favorite Outline of
ROBERT C. GRAY, Pastor
Trinity Baptist Church
Jacksonville, Florida

"THIS MAN"

The master hand of the Holy Spirit is constantly arresting our attention and pointing Jesus out to us as "this man" in the Word of God by some glowing sentence or startling truth— some pointed declaration or dynamic word such as "Behold!"

With that in mind, let us study seven verses of Scripture that deal with the Man, Christ Jesus:

I. **"Never man spoke like this man" (John 7:46).**
   In John 7:44-45 we read that the officers who were sent to arrest Jesus were asked why they hadn't brought Him. They had heard Jesus' words and were, as it were, handcuffed by them, and consequently could not put handcuffs on Jesus. The words that Jesus spoke were arresting words—words of power, words that assured the officers that they were not dealing with the average person.

II. **"This man receiveth sinners" (Luke 15:2).**
   Jesus Christ, the Son of God, came into this world to seek and to save that which was lost (Luke 19:10). He came to give His life a ransom for many (Matt. 20:28). Yes, Jesus was a friend to sinners, and He received sinners, He ate with sinners. "This man" is still receiving sinners. He is ready to receive you, and to forgive your sins if you will by faith receive Him (John 1:12-13).

III. **"I find no fault in this man" (Luke 23:4).**
   In John's Gospel (18:38 and 19:4, 6), Pilate admits three times that Jesus is faultless. Yes, Jesus is faultless. He is

40

sinless (II Cor. 5:21; Heb. 4:15; I John 3:5). He came to pay the debt of sin and He paid it in full.

IV. **"Through this man is preached unto you the forgiveness of sins" (Acts 13:38).**

Jesus is the only one who can forgive sins. The message is "through this man," not through church membership; not through shaking the preacher's hand; not through being immersed in water; not through living a good life; and not through doing the very best you know how. There is no other way. Our sins are forgiven for Christ's sake (Eph. 4:32).

V. **"This man . . . offered one sacrifice for sins . . ." (Heb. 10:12).**

Jesus offered one offering—Himself—and He offered this offering once, for all, forever. Thank God for the spotless, sinless offering—Jesus! "The blood of Jesus Christ his Son cleanseth us from all sin" (I John 1:7).

VI. **"He [God] will judge the world in righteousness by [that] man whom he hath ordained" (Acts 17:31).**

I am so glad that God had oppointed "this man" to judge the quick and the dead (John 5:22; Acts 10:42; Rev. 20:11-15). Therefore, I have no fear of the judgment.

VII. **"Truly this man was the Son of God" (Mark 15:39).**

Jesus evidenced a personality that none else could produce or reveal. He was God in flesh. He was the fullness of the Godhead in flesh. He came to do the will of God the Father, and in every minute detail of His living, His service, and His death He did only the will of the heavenly Father. No other man has ever lived upon this earth who completely satisfied the Father in every detail of his life.

In summary "He was, He is, the Son of God!" Thank God for "this man." If you do not know Him, let me urge you one more time, receive "this man" as your personal Savior, and do it this moment!

Read John 1:12-13; 3:16, 18, 36; 5:24; Romans 10:9-10; Ephesians 2:8-9; Titus 3:5. "Believe on the Lord Jesus Christ and thou shalt be saved" (Acts 16:31).

The Favorite Outline of
OLIVER B. GREENE

THE BLESSINGS OF OUR SALVATION
Ephesians 1:3-14

I. God the Father planned our salvation (vv. 3-6).

A. He has blessed us (v. 3).
  1. The originator of the blessing: "Father."
  2. The recipient of the blessing: "us."
  3. The nature of the blessing: "all spiritual blessings."
  4. The location of the blessing: "in heavenly places in Christ."

B. He has chosen us (v. 4).
  1. The nature of the choice: "chosen for himself."
  2. The object of the choice: "us."
  3. The sphere of the choice: "in him."
  4. The time of the choice: "before the foundation of the world."
  5. The purpose of the choice: "that we should be holy and without blame before him in love."

C. He has predestinated us (vv. 5-6a).
  1. The meaning of predestination: "predestinated."
  2. The object of predestination: "us."
  3. The purpose of predestination: "unto the adoption of children by Jesus Christ to himself."
  4. The standard of predestination: "according to the good pleasure of his will."
  5. The goal of predestination: "to the praise of the glory of his grace."

D. He has accepted us (v. 6b).
  1. The object of acceptance: "us."
  2. The sphere of acceptance: "in the beloved."

43

II. God the Son paid for our salvation (vv. 7-12).

A. He redeemed us (v. 7a).
1. The possession of redemption: "we have."
2. The means of redemption: "through his blood."
B. He forgave us (v. 7b).
1. The area of forgiveness: "sins."
2. The standard of forgiveness: "according to the riches of his grace."
C. He revealed His will to us (vv. 8-10).
1. The sphere of revelation: "in all wisdom and prudence."
2. The object of revelation: "the mystery of his will."
3. The standard of revelation: "according to his good pleasure which he hath purposed in himself."
4. The goal of revelation: "that in the dispensation of the fullness of times he might gather together in one all things in Christ, both which are in heaven, and which are on earth."
D. He inherited us (vv. 11-12).
1. The nature of inheritance: "we were obtained as an inheritance."
2. The sphere of inheritance: "in whom."
3. The standard of inheritance: "being predestinated according to the purpose of him who worketh all things after the counsel of his own will."
4. The goal of inheritance: "that we should be to the praise of his glory."

III. God the Spirit protects our salvation (vv. 13-14).

A. He seals us (v. 13).
1. The object of sealing: "ye."
2. The time of sealing: "when ye believed."
3. The nature of sealing: "the holy Spirit of promise."

B. He serves as our earnest (v. 14).
   1. The meaning of the earnest: "down payment."
   2. The area of the earnest: "of our inheritance."
   3. The duration of the earnest: "until the redemption of the purchased possession."
   4. The goal of the earnest: "unto the praise of his glory."

The Favorite Outline of
ROBERT GROMACKI
Cedarville, Ohio

WHY MEMORIZE THE SCRIPTURES

Proverbs 3:3-4

"Let not mercy and truth forsake thee: bind them about thy neck; write them upon the table of thine heart: so shalt thou find favour and good understanding in the sight of God and man."

Deep down in the heart of every normal person born into the human race there is a threefold desire: a desire to be happy; a desire to be wise; and a desire to be successful. Anyone who will schedule himself to obey Joshua 1:8; Psalm 1:2-3; 37:4; and James 1:5 will realize this in his life.

Why should we memorize the sacred Scriptures?

I. It is a command from God (Deut. 6:6-7; Job 22:22). We should obey Him because:
   A. He is our creator (John 1:3, 10).
      1. We are the sheep of His pasture (Ps. 100:3).
      2. Our breath is in His hands (Dan. 5:23).
   B. He is our redeemer (Rev. 5:9).
      1. We are His purchased possession (I Cor. 6:20; I Peter 1:18-19).
      2. We are not our own (I Cor. 6:19).

II. Wisdom is promised: "good understanding in the sight of God and man" (Prov. 3:4).
   A. Heavenly wisdom is far better than earthly wealth (Prov. 8:11).

46

B. Solomon discovered that:
1. the ways of wisdom are pleasant (v. 17; see also vv. 13-16, 18).
2. the paths of wisdom are peace (v. 17; James 3:17).

III. Success is promised (Josh. 1:8; Psalm 1:3).
A. Moody arose at 4:00 A.M. to meditate in the Scriptures.
B. Spurgeon, someone said, spent three hours a day studying the Scriptures.
C. Dr. Jack Van Impe is one of the most successful men living today. He has the entire New Testament committed to memory.

IV. Answered prayer is promised (John 15:7).
Definite answered prayers are only for those who please God (I John 3:22).

V. Spiritual cleansing is promised (Ps. 119:9; John 15:3; II Cor. 7:1; Eph. 5:26).

VI. Protection is promised.
A. From sin (Ps. 119:11).
B. From Satan (Matt. 4:3-10; I John 2:14).
C. From strange women (Prov. 6:21-33).
D. From strange doctrines (Eph. 4:14).

VII. Soul saving is promised (Ps. 126:6; James 1:18, 21; I Peter 1:23).

Therefore, "Let the Word of Christ dwell in you richly . . . " (Col. 3:16).

The Favorite Outline of
J. O. GROOMS, President
Treasure Path to Soul Winning, Inc.
Lynchburg, Virginia

IN DAYS LIKE THESE

II Peter 3

Second Peter is an epistle of crisis. A crisis is a period of transition when the present order and arrangement of things passes away and a new order is ushered in. This is the kind of a period the Church has been living in from Pentecost to the present. Christ left the Church with the hope of His return when He said, "I will come again" (John 14:3). To enable believers to confront seeming hesitation or haste in the fulfillment of this event, Peter presents a series of guidelines in the third chapter of this epistle.

I. **In days like these God's people need to remember again the message of the Word of God (II Peter 3:1-2).** This message covers human sin and failure, and the only hope for men is the salvation provided by God at Christ's coming.
   A. Remembrance extends to the Old Testament, "the words which were spoken before by the holy prophets."
   B. Remembrance includes the New Testament, "the commandment of us the apostles."

II. **In days like these God's people need to recognize the false teaching of the false teachers (II Peter 3:3-7).**
   A. The fallacious reasoning of false teachers (vv. 3-4). The false teachers argue on the basis of a limited period of investigation that there has been no crisis in the past, and there will be no crisis in the future as was introduced by the coming of Christ.

48

B. The absolute refutation of this reasoning (vv. 5-7). Peter points out that there was a flood in the past as set forth in Genesis, and the same Word of God points to a crisis in the future.

III. **In days like these God's people need to realize that the movements of God cannot be measured over the patterns of men (II Peter 3:8-10).** Inasmuch as the coming of Christ has been long delayed there are some who charge God with being slack in carrying out His promise. The answer is twofold. If there seems to be hesitation it should be remembered that:
   A. The schedule God follows is totally different from that of men (v. 8).
   B. God wants to harvest a full crop of souls, so He is letting sufficient time elapse for men to accept the provision in Christ (v. 9).

IV. **In days like these God's people need to respond with steadfastness of faith and holiness of conduct (II Peter 3:11-18).**
   A. The negative encouragement for faith and holiness is simply that this is the only way to survive the coming crisis (vv. 11, 14, 17).
   B. The positive approach is the deep longing for the coming of the new order in which righteousness will settle down and be at home (vv. 12, 13, 18).
   C. Therefore we are to "grow in grace, and in the knowledge of our Lord and Saviour Jesus Christ" (v. 18).

The Favorite Outline of
HERMAN A. HOYT, President
Grace Schools
Winona Lake, Indiana

RESPONSIBLE LIVING

I Thessalonians 1

The Declaration of Independence of the United States tells us "that all men are created equal, that they are endowed by their Creator with certain unalienable Rights, that among these are Life, Liberty and the pursuit of Happiness." For every right there is a corresponding responsibility. If life is an inalienable right received from God, then we are accountable to God to live responsible lives.

The business of life is to live—to live righteously, reasonably, and responsibly. But this age knows almost everything about life except how to live it. Unprincipled, unrestrained, restless, and reckless living characterizes our times.

In I Thessalonians 1 we have what has been referred to as a model church. As we look at this ancient assembly, this fine fellowship, we find that they knew what responsible living in an irresponsible age was all about.

I. Responsible living is positional living.
". . . the church of the Thessalonians which is in God the Father and in the Lord Jesus Christ" (I Thess. 1:1). In Christ we have:
- A. Acceptance which can never be reversed (Eph. 1:6).
- B. Assurance which can never be revoked (John 10:28-29).

II. Responsible living is patterned living.
"And ye became followers of us, and of the Lord . . . " (I Thess. 1:6-7).
- A. The pattern of the apostles of the Lord: "Ye became followers of us" (I Thess. 2:9-10).

B. The pattern of the Lord of the apostles—"and of the Lord."

III. Responsible living is principled living.
"... how ye turned to God from idols ..." (I Thess. 1:9).
A. They took a stand for something: "turned to God."
B. They took a stand against something: "turned ... from idols."

IV. Responsible living is purposeful living.
"For from you sounded out the word of the Lord ..." (I Thess. 1:8). Oh, the emptiness, aimlessness, and shamefulness of a purposeless life! For the Thessalonians, purposeful living was:
A. Serving the Lord: "to serve" (v. 9; see also Luke 1:74).
B. Seeking the lost: "sounded out the word" (v. 8; see also Luke 19:10).

V. Responsible living is prepared living.
"And to wait for his Son from heaven ..." (I Thess. 1:10). They lived positional, purposeful, principled, and patterned lives so that they would be prepared when He came.
A. We should be prepared for the appearance of Christ (I John 2:28).
B. We should be prepared for an accounting to Christ (I Cor. 3:13).

The responsible life is the life that is "hid with Christ in God"; the life that is "conformed to the image of his Son"; the life that is uncompromising in principle; the life that is sacrificial in service; and the life that is ready to be "caught up ... in the clouds to meet the Lord in the air."

The Favorite Outline of
J. DON JENNINGS,
International Director of Enrichment
and Evangelism, ABWE, Inc.
Atlanta, Georgia

51

YOU CAN BE SURE OF THIS

I have heard people say, "You can't be sure of anything today."
J. B. Priestly said, "In this atomic age we are sure of nothing
but sex." An old saying known by many is, "You can be sure
of only two things: death and taxes." In this message I want
to speak of three things you can be sure of.

I. **You can be sure of the Scriptures.**
"The law of the Lord is perfect, converting the soul: the
testimony of the Lord is sure, making wise the simple"
(Ps. 19:7). "The testimony of the Lord" refers to the
Scriptures, the Word of God. Peter assures us concerning the Scriptures: "We have also a more sure word of
prophecy . . ." (II Peter 1:19).

A. The spade says we can be sure. The testimony of the
spade has confirmed the accuracy of the Bible, as
archaeologists have checked more than twenty-five
thousand sites of Bible lands and found thousands
of clay documents in the cuneiform script, dating
from about 3300 B.C. to A.D. 50. Norman L. Geisler
and William E. Nix, in their book *A General Intro-
duction to the Bible,* stated: "No area of modern
science has confirmed the historicity and authenticity of the Scriptures so much as has archaeology,"
and archaeologist Nelson Glueck said, "No archae-
ological discovery has ever controverted a Biblical
reference."

B. The Scriptures say we can be sure. The Bible says of
itself: all Scripture is inspired of God (II Tim. 3:16),
is perfect (Ps. 19:7), permanent (Ps. 119:89), and has

been given by God through holy men of God as they were inspired by the Holy Spirit (II Peter 1:21). Rene Pache commented: "As for the Bible itself, it reiterates throughout that it *is* the Word of God. The Old Testament repeats 3,808 times such synonymous expressions as, 'Jehovah saith,' 'thus saith Jehovah,' and 'the word of God came saying. . . .' "

C. The Savior says we can be sure. Jesus Christ said of the Bible: ". . . the Scripture cannot be broken" (John 10:35); ". . . thy word is truth" (John 17:17); "Till heaven and earth pass, one jot or one tittle shall in no wise pass from the law, till all be fulfilled" (Matt. 5:18); "Heaven and earth shall pass away: but my words shall not pass away" (Mark 13:31); "He that rejected me, and receiveth not my words, hath one that judgeth him: the word that I have spoken, the same shall judge him in the last day" (John 12:48). In his book, *The Saviour and the Scriptures,* Robert P. Lightner summarizes concerning Christ's teaching about inspiration: "The significance of His [Christ's] view of the God-breathed Scriptures results in His acceptance of their total inerrancy, absolute infallibility, authenticity, genuineness, authority and credibility." The Bible claims to be and proves to be the sure Word of God.

II. You can be sure of sin.

God's sure Word warns: ". . . be sure your sin will find you out" (Num. 32:23). You can be sure your sin will find you out in:

A. Your body (Job 20:11; Gal. 6:7-8).
B. Your conscience (I Tim. 4:2).
C. Your children (Exod. 34:6-7).
D. Your character (Prov. 5:22).
E. A wasted life (Rom. 8:8).
F. Judgment (Heb. 9:27; Rev. 20:11-15).
G. Hell forever (Ps. 9:17; Rev. 14:11; 21:8).

53

III. You can be sure of salvation.

God exhorts us: ". . . give diligence to make your calling and election sure . . ." (II Peter 1:10). This means we are to make sure we are saved. Thank God, you can be sure of salvation.

A. By the Word of God (I John 5:9-13).
B. By the witness of God (Rom. 8:16; I John 3:24; 4:13; 5:10).
C. By the works of God (II Cor. 5:17; Eph. 2:10; I John 2:3-5, 29; 3:9, 14; 5:4-5).

If you are not sure of salvation, repent of your sins and believe on the Lord Jesus Christ right now (Luke 13:3; John 3:16; Acts 20:21), then you will have the witness of God, the Holy Spirit, who will enable you to do the works of God. You can be *sure* of this.

The Favorite Outline of
CARL JOHNSON, Evangelist
Beckley, West Virginia

GRACE

Hebrews 4:16

Often expounded; never exhausted.

I. Sovereign grace.
"Let us therefore come boldly unto the throne of grace, that we may obtain mercy, and find grace to help in time of need" (Heb. 4:16).

II. Saving grace.
"For by grace are ye saved through faith; and that not of yourselves: it is the gift of God: not of works, lest any man should boast" (Eph. 2:8-9).

III. Schooling grace.
"For the grace of God that bringeth salvation hath appeared to all men, teaching us that, denying ungodliness and worldly lusts, we should live soberly, righteously, and godly, in this present world; looking for that blessed hope, and the glorious appearing of the great God and our Saviour Jesus Christ" (Titus 2:11-13).

IV. Sufficient grace.
"And he said unto me, My grace is sufficient for thee: for my strength is made perfect in weakness. Most gladly therefore will I rather glory in my infirmities, that the power of Christ may rest upon me" (II Cor. 12:9).

V. Sustaining grace.
"Who hath saved us, and called us with an holy calling, not according to our works, but according to his own

purpose and grace, which was given us in Christ Jesus before the world began" (II Tim. 1:9).

VI. Supplying grace.

"And God is able to make all grace abound toward you; that ye, always having all sufficiency in all things, may abound to every good work" (II Cor. 9:8).

VII. Surpassing grace.

"That in the ages to come he might shew the exceeding riches of his grace in his kindness toward us through Christ Jesus" (Eph. 2:7).

The Favorite Outline of
JIMMY JOHNSON
Fuquay-Varina, North Carolina

VESSELS UNTO HONOR OR DISHONOR

II Timothy 2:20-21

When I read these verses, immediately one question pricks my mind: Am I a vessel unto honor or a vessel unto dishonor? Paul saw himself as a "chosen vessel"; David envisioned his life as a "potter's vessel"; Isaiah emphasized the "clean vessel"; and Peter preached on the "weaker vessel."

What are the ingredients in the recipe of the God-pleasing, Christ-honoring "honorable vessel?"

I. **An honorable vessel is a saved vessel (gold and silver vs. wood and earth, v. 20).**
   A. Saved and you know (II Tim. 1:12).
   B. Saved and you show (I Peter 2:9).
   C. Saved and you grow (I Peter 2:2).

II. **An honorable vessel is a sanctified vessel ("sanctified," v. 21).**
   A. Sanctified positionally (I Cor. 6:11).
   B. Sanctified progressively (I Thess. 4:3-4).
   C. Sanctified potentially (Jude 24).

III. **An honorable vessel is a surrendered vessel ("meet [fitting] for the master's use," v. 21).**
   A. Surrendered to a Person (Rom. 12:1-2).
   B. Surrendered to a program (Matt. 28:19-20).
   C. Surrendered to a plan (Prov. 3:5-6).

IV. An honorable vessel is a skilled vessel ("prepared unto every good work," v. 21).
   A. Skilled in the Word (II Tim. 2:15).
   B. Skilled in witnessing (I Peter 3:15).
   C. Skilled in the work (II Tim. 3:16-17).

The Favorite Outline of
BOB KELLEY, Evangelist
Chattanooga, Tennessee

THE CHRIST OF THE CROSS

I Corinthians 15:3-6

   I. The Christ: "Christ" (I Cor. 15:3).

  II. The curse: "died for our sins" (I Cor. 15:3).

 III. The complement: "he was buried . . . he rose again" (I Cor. 15:4).

 IV. The confirmation: "he was seen of Cephas, then of the twelve . . . , of above five hundred brethren at once" (I Cor. 15:5-6).

  V. The contemporary: "he ever liveth to make intercession for them" (Heb. 7:25; see also Rev. 1:18).

 VI. The consummation: "because I live, ye shall live also" (John 14:19b).

VII. The constraint: "For the love of Christ constraineth us; because we thus judge, that if one died for all, then were all dead: and that he died for all, that they which live should not henceforth live unto themselves, but unto him which died for them, and rose again" (II Cor. 5:14-15).

The Favorite Outline of
ROBERT G. LEE, Pastor Emeritus
Bellevue Baptist Church
Memphis, Tennessee

THE NEW BIRTH

John 3:1-18

George Whitefield was asked why he preached so often on
"Ye must be born again." He answered, "Because ye must be
born again." Have *you* been born again? Without it you have
no hope of escaping the terrors of hell or enjoying the glories
of heaven. The Lord Jesus said, "Ye must be born again"
(John 3:7). God wants you to become His child through the
new birth.

I. What the new birth is not.
  A. Religion—Nicodemus a Pharisee, was very reli-
     gious (v. 10).
  B. Resolution—to keep the law (Gal. 2:16) or to live a
     moral life (Eph. 2:8-9).
  C. Reformation—man's trouble is on the inside. He
     needs inward regeneration, not outward refor-
     mation (Titus 3:5).

II. What the new birth is.
  A. It is like the wind, a mystery that cannot be ex-
     plained, but a reality that cannot be denied (v. 8).
  B. It is receiving God's nature and becoming God's
     child (II Peter 1:4).
  C. It is the beginning of a new life (II Cor. 5:17).

III. Why you must be born again.
  A. The Lord Jesus Christ said so (v. 7).
  B. You need God's nature in order to enjoy God's
     heaven.

IV. How to be born again.

A. It is "not of blood" (John 1:13). You are not a Christian because your parents are.

B. "Nor of the will of the flesh" (John 1:13). You are not a Christian by your own efforts.

C. "Nor of the will of man" (John 1:13). No other man can make you a Christian.

D. "But of God" (John 1:13). You must be born "of the Spirit" (John 3:5).

E. Your part is to receive Christ who died and arose for your sins (John 1:12; 3:14-18; I Peter 2:24; 3:18).

V. When to be born again.

Now! Before it is eternally too late (Prov. 27:1; James 4:13-15).

The Favorite Outline of
PAUL J. LEVIN, Evangelist
Carlock, Illinois

REACHING THE NORM OF SPIRITUAL LIFE

Psalm 119

Every growing Christian encounters difficulty transmitting into practical experience what he so readily accepts mentally as being the truth of God. Psalm 119 gives us the most comprehensive coverage of this matter, if not the most vivid and dramatic.

I. The possibility portrayed.
A. The examples displayed (vv. 1-3).
B. The exhortation discovered (v. 4).
C. The experience desired (v. 5).

II. The probability pondered.
A. The inevitable question (v. 9; see also John 3:9).
B. The inferred doubt (v. 10b).
C. The induced precaution (v. 11).

III. The petitions presented.
A. The cry for mercy (v. 17)
B. The cry for vision (v. 18).
C. The cry for remembrance (v. 19).
D. The cry for satisfaction (v. 20).

IV. The problem preventing.
A. The deterrent of the soul (v. 25).
B. The dullness of the mind (v. 27).
C. The deception of the heart (v. 29).

V. The preplexity provoked.
A. The depth of deception (v. 35).

B. The lack of affection (v. 36).
C. The fear of deflection (v. 37).
D. The plea for direction (vv. 37b-38).

VI. The proper perspective.
A. The prelude to victory (v. 57).
B. The pleasure of victory (v. 63).
C. The proof of victory (v. 112).

VII. The pathway of progress.
A. The reflection—facts (vv. 58-60).
B. The refinement—fire (vv. 69, 83, 85-86).
C. The reassurance—faith (vv. 97, 103, 105, 111).

All the demons of hell are committed to the proposition that no lost sinner shall see the simplicity of salvation. When one is saved from this delusion, Satan shifts his attack to make the abundant life appear utterly impossible.

The Favorite Outline of
S. FRANKLIN LOGSDON
Largo, Florida

THE TWO MOST IMPORTANT LITTLE WORDS
IN THE ENGLISH LANGUAGE—DO RIGHT

One of the sayings of Dr. Bob Jones, Sr. was "Do right. Do right if the stars fall." There is never a time when it is right to do wrong. It is always right to do right. It is never right to do wrong even to get a chance to do right.

It is right that people should be saved. It is right that saved people should get baptized. Church membership is right. It is right to tithe. It is right to win souls to Jesus.

In Mark 10:17-27 is the story of a young man about whom many things were right, but who, in the end, made a tragic, wrong choice.

  I. **He came to the right person: Jesus.**
    A. He slighted the deity of Christ: "Good Master" (v. 17).
    B. Jesus loved him and dealt tenderly (v.21).

 II. **He came in the right way.**
    A. Running (v. 17).
    B. Kneeling (v. 17).

III. **He asked the right question.**
    "What shall I do that I may inherit eternal life?" (v. 17). This is the most important question in the world.

IV. **He got the right answer (vv. 19-21).**
    A. Six commandments.
      1. Jesus left out four.

2. Commandments are not the way of salvation.
B. "All these have I observed" (v. 20).
   1. He was a good young man.
   2. "What lack I yet" (Matt. 19:20).
C. "Follow me" (v. 21).
   1. Sell what you have.
   2. Take up the cross.

V. He made a wrong choice.
A. He was sad.
B. He was grieved.

The Favorite Outline of
BUD LYLES, Evangelist
Brownsburg, Indiana

TOO GOOD FOR HEAVEN

Romans 9:30–10:4

The Bible declares that the Jews in Paul's day were "too good" for heaven! They were so righteous in their own sight that they would not turn to Jesus for salvation. The same is true of countless millions today.

I. Three people who were "too good" for heaven.
A. A religious man (John 3:1-7).
1. This man fasted, prayed, gave alms, was very religious and probably lived a clean life.
2. Religion has never saved one soul. Anyone who worships anything is religious. Thousands of Americans now worship Satan!
B. A moral man (Luke 18:9-14).
1. When people get saved they become moral (II Cor. 5:17).
2. Morality will keep you out of a lot of trouble, but not out of hell.
C. A confessing man (Matt. 7:21-23).
1. This is a prophetic event.
2. Some use this to support the "falling from grace" doctrine. Jesus said, "I *never* knew you."
3. This man was depending on his "wonderful works."

II. Three people who were "good enough" for heaven.
A. A thief (Luke 23:39-43).
The repentant thief acknowledged that he deserved

to be on the cross, yet Jesus said he would go to paradise that very day.
- B. An adulterous woman (John 4:7-42)
  This woman had lived a life of loose morals. After meeting Jesus she was saved and became a soul-winner.
- C. A crooked tax collector (Luke 18:9-14).
  He would not even look up toward heaven, but he walked out of the temple justified.

III. What lessons can we learn?
- A. We have no righteousness of our own (Rom. 3:10).
- B. Only Jesus is righteous (II Cor. 5:21a).
- C. Those who look to themselves, their religion, or their works for salvation will face God with a righteousness that is as filthy rags (Isa. 64:6).
- D. Only those who receive Jesus are righteous in God's sight (II Cor. 5:21b).

Receive Jesus as your Savior today (John 1:12).

The Favorite Outline of
JIM LYONS, Evangelist
Garland, Texas

CHRISTIANS—BE READY

I Peter 3:15

"But sanctify the Lord God in your hearts: and be ready always to give an answer to every man that asketh you a reason of the hope that is in you with meekness and fear."

I want you to notice with me not only this great passage of Scripture, but others in the New Testament that have to do with Christians being ready. You say, Ready for what? Ready for anything; for the unexpected. Always ready—the readiness of a Christian. There are many verses in the Bible that deal with this. The Bible speaks at least seven times of things that a Christian should be ready for or ways that a Christian should be ready.

I. Ready for the coming of the Lord.

The Bible plainly teaches that "to be ready always" means to be ready for the coming of the Lord. The Bible puts nearly as much emphasis on His Second Coming as it does on His First Coming.

More than once during His lifetime on earth Jesus said that those who are saved should be ready for His Second Coming. For instance, Matthew 24:44 says, "Therefore be ye also ready: for in such an hour as ye think not the Son of man cometh."

A ready Christian is one who is ready for the coming of the Lord, Jesus Christ. I wonder if the truth were

really known, how many of God's people would be
ready for the coming of the Lord.

II. Ready to work.

One who is ready should be ready to work. Oh, my,
what an ugly word! Ready to work. Christians often
avoid this topic by saying, "Well, let's talk about
something doctrinal, something for Sunday." "Work"
is for Monday through Saturday. Yet the Bible says
in Titus 3:1, "Put them in mind to be subject to princi-
palities and powers, to obey magistrates, to be ready
to every good work." Here Paul is writing to Titus,
pastor of a church on the Isle of Crete.

A church that is not a working church is not a New
Testament church, regardless of what its doctrine is.
To be New Testament, it is not only what you believe,
but what you do.

III. Ready to die.

The Bible teaches that Christian readiness involves a
readiness to die. We should be ready to die. Paul said
in II Timothy 4:6, "For I am now ready to be offered,
and the time of my departure is at hand." Paul was
ready to die.

In Acts 21:13 (long before he ever wrote Timothy) Paul
says "What mean ye to weep and to break mine heart?
for I am ready not to be bound only, but also to die at
Jerusalem for the name of the Lord Jesus."

IV. Ready to preach the gospel.

A Christian should always be ready to preach the
gospel. In Romans 1:14-16 Paul used three brief state-
ments that express a tremendous purpose of his life:
"I am debtor," "I am ready," and "I am not ashamed."
Paul felt that he had a great debt. First of all he felt an
indebtedness to God. Every Christian ought to feel that

they absolutely owe God their entire life. People who feel this indebtedness will be ready to preach. The world needs people who are called to preach the gospel and whose lives are devoted to making the Word of God known, There is a sense in which every Christian is a preacher.

V. Ready to give to the Lord.
The Bible teaches that every Christian should be ready to give to the Lord. I am talking about material things. It says in I Timothy 6:17-18, "Charge them that are rich in this world, that they be not high-minded, nor trust in uncertain riches, but in the living God, who giveth us richly all things to enjoy; that they do good, that they be rich in good works, ready to distribute, willing to communicate." This is one of the most blessed and wonderful things in the life of a Christian, not something to fear or be selfish about, but ready to do always.

VI. Ready mind.
The Bible speaks of a ready mind. It says in I Peter 5:2, "Feed the flock of God which is among you, taking the oversight thereof, not by constraint, but willingly; not for filthy lucre, but of a ready mind." This is having a mind always ready to do the will and work of God.

VII. Ready to speak for Jesus.
A ready Christian is always ready to speak for Jesus, always ready to give a testimony for the Lord at every opportunity. "But sanctify the Lord God in your hearts: be ready always to give an answer to every man that asketh you a reason of the hope that is in you with meekness and fear" (I Peter 3:15).

Christian, are you ready? My prayer for you is that you will "be a vessel unto honour, sanctified, and meet for the master's use and prepared unto every good work" (II Tim. 2:21).

Sinner, my prayer for you is that you will heed God's command, "Prepare to meet thy God" (Amos 4:12) by "repentance toward God, and faith toward our Lord Jesus Christ" (Acts 20:21) and be ready for anything.

The Favorite Outline of
TOM MALONE, Pastor
Emmanuel Baptist Church
Pontiac, Michigan

THE RESULTS OF JUSTIFICATION

Romans 5:1-11

Justification means to be "accounted righteous, and treated so" by God.

The *source* of justification is God's grace (Rom. 3:24).

The *basis* of justification is the blood of Christ (Rom. 5:9).

The *guarantee* of justification is the resurrection of Christ (Rom. 4:25).

The *channel* of justification is faith (Rom. 5:1).

"Being justified by faith, we have":

I. Peace.

"We have peace with God through our Lord Jesus Christ" (v. 1; see also Ps. 85:10; Eph. 2:14, 17; Col. 1:20-21).

II. Position.

"This grace wherein we stand" (v. 2; see also I Cor. 15:1; Eph. 1:6; I John 4:17b).

III. Prospect.

We "rejoice in hope of the glory of God" (v. 2; see also Rom. 8:23-25; Titus 2:13; I John 3:2-3).

IV. Purpose.

"Tribulation worketh patience; and patience, experience; and experience, hope" (vv. 3-4; see also Rom. 8:28-30; II Tim. 1:9; James. 1:3).

V. Power.

"The Holy Ghost which is given to us" (v. 5; see also Zech. 4:6b; Acts 1:8; Eph. 3:16-19).

VI. Pardon.

"We shall be saved from wrath through him" (v. 9; see also John 3:36; Rom. 1:18; I Thess. 5:9).

VII. Provision.

"We shall be saved by his [resurrection] life" (v. 10; see also Rom. 8:33-34; II Cor. 9:8; Heb. 7:25; 9:24).

All these blessings become ours the moment we exercise faith in our Lord Jesus Christ (v. 1).

The Favorite Outline of
JOHN B. MARCHBANKS
Greenville, South Carolina

THE LORD'S TRUE SERVANTS

Mark 11:1-11

The message that I wish to bring is about God's true servants. The question could be asked, "What kind of servants would the Lord choose to send on an errand?" Let us see from our text what kind of servants the Lord sent.

I. They were converted (v. 1)

They were called disciples, true followers of the Lord. Jesus said, "Except ye be converted, and become as little children, ye shall not enter into the kingdom of heaven" (Matt. 18:3).

II. They were consecrated (vv. 2, 4).

In verse 2 Jesus said, "Go." In verse 4 we read, "they went." They went immediately, with no questions asked. I would call that consecration. I think that two of the greatest verses having to do with what I am talking about are found in Romans 12:1-2. The Lord desires that His children walk, talk, look, smell, and act like His children.

III. They were courageous (vv. 4-7).

When they were questioned about taking the colt in verse 5, they showed great boldness and said what Jesus had commanded. We need to be brave in these perilous times. Those who are filled with the Spirit are courageous (Acts 4:13).

IV. They were consistent (vv. 4-7).

They let nothing take them off on a tangent; without

wavering they delivered the colt to Jesus. There is positively no excuse for not serving the Lord consistently. Let us be consistent (I Cor. 15:58).

V. They were concerned (v. 7).

They were concerned about bringing the colt to Jesus. The colt is like a lost sinner. It was tied, as the sinner is by sin. The colt was "by the door . . . where two ways met." So is the sinner—near enough to be saved, and faced with two ways: the broad and the narrow (Matt. 7:13-14). Our main objective should be to get the sinner to Jesus.

My prayer for you is that you will be one of the Lord's true servants: converted, consecrated, courageous, consistent, and concerned.

The Favorite Outline of
LEON F. MAURER
Terre Haute, Indiana

SEVEN Cs OF CHRISTIAN LIBERTY

Luke 1:74-75

"He is not escaped who drags his chain" (French proverb).

I. The conception of liberty.

The frightful fact, everywhere evident, is that man is a groveling slave, subject not primarily to establishments and systems but subject to sin. "Every one that committeth sin is the bondservant of sin" (John 8:34, ASV). "He is a free man whom the truth makes free, and all are slaves besides" (Cowper).

II. The call to liberty.

"Behold, now is the acceptable time" (now is the jubilee of your release), "behold, now is the day of salvation" (II Cor. 6:2, ASV). The call of Christ is not tomorrow, but today. "Today, if ye will hear his voice, harden not your hearts" (Heb. 3:15).

III. The condition of liberty.

The jubilee proclamation was that of a full and free liberation for all sorts and conditions of men. Our gospel liberty, however, through a gift of utterly free grace, is granted only upon a certain condition. In our salvation Christ asks not for our decision, but for our submission, submission to Him as Lord (Rom. 10:9-10). The simple and single condition of liberty, paradoxical as it may seem, is through complete captivity to Christ.

IV. The courage of liberty.

We ordinarily associate courage with fleshly boldness

and natural bravery. But the courage of Christian liberty is something different, something superior, something divine. It has a holy carefreeness that is basic to true fearlessness. Consider the boldness of the three Hebrew young men (Daniel 3:16-18). And what did they lose in the fire? Nothing but their bondage.

V. The contagion of liberty.

The world senses whether we possess real freedom. Our very features betray either freedom or fear (Acts 4:13). Do people pant for the liberty you possess? Has God so emancipated your soul from fear that you manifest the freedom that is contagious for Christ?

VI. The confines of liberty.

Ours is no false freedom. It has its sacred confines. We have liberty indeed—to be holy, to do right, to do the will of God. David expressed this true freedom in Psalm 119:45, "I will walk at liberty [Heb. at large]: for I seek thy precepts." Christ Himself lived within the confines of heaven's law. Was He in bondage? or did He dutifully delight in the freedom of God's will?

VII. The contributions of liberty.

Our gospel freedom is never to make us independent and lawless, but frees us that we may "by love serve." The great apostle said, "Though I be free from all men, yet have I made myself servant unto all" (I Cor. 9:19). He deliberately and of his own volition made himself servant of all men that he could gain for them this gospel freedom.

We have been liberated, not merely for our *enjoyment*, but for our *employment*.

> *The Favorite Outline of*
> L. E. MAXWELL, President
> Prairie Bible Institute
> Three Hills, Alberta, Canada

DELIVERANCE FROM DEMONISM

Mark 5:1-20

The demon-possessed man is used by Christ Jesus to warn about the final state of everyone in a lost eternity. Sin reached its climax in this man. Everyone in lost eternity (hell; the lake of fire—Rev. 21:8) will be under demon control and in worse condition than this man.

I. What sin and Satan did for him.
   A. Robbed him of manhood, self-respect, decency, home, salvation.
   B. Demonized him—the name "Legion" indicated from two thousand to six thousand demons.

II. What the world did for him.
   A. Lectured, scolded, exhorted him.
   B. Chained, institutionalized him.
   C. Did not (could not) cure him.

III. What he did for himself.
   A. Ran to Jesus personally, immediately, sincerely.
   B. Ran to Jesus just as he was—despite sin and demonism manipulating his tongue, saying, "What have we to do with thee?"

IV. What Jesus did for him.
   A. Imparted a right mind, God-pleasing thinking.
   B. Clothed him. Physical clothing illustrates being clothed with God's righteousness, as described in Romans 3:21-26.
   C. Imparted a new nature—he was born again (John

3:1-16). Evidenced by his desire to fellowship with Jesus.
D. Gave him a new work to do—witness to loved ones and everyone affected by his life.
  1. Many souls saved and Christians spiritually strengthened.
  2. Past, present, and future fruitage was beyond human comprehension by Christ's work in and through him, and through Scripture describing his salvation.

The Favorite Outline of
WILLIAM R. McCARRELL, Director
Christian Work Center
Cicero, Illinois

PAUL'S PASSION FOR SOULS

Romans 10

Someone has well said, "A Christian not burdened for souls is a poor likeness of Christ." In Romans 10 we see such a burden.

I. Paul's desire (v. 1).

His concern and passion for souls is evident. His desire is coupled with a "prayer to God" (v. 1). No prayer—no power. No supplication—no strength. No cry—no courage. See the tears of Paul in Acts 20:19 and of David in Psalm 126:5-6.

II. Paul's discernment (vv. 2-3).

He knew that even highly religious folk were lost without Christ. Zealous but ignorant. Attempting to establish their own righteousness they thus did not have the righteousness of God. "Ye will not come to me" (John 5:40).

III. Paul's devotion (v. 4).

"Christ is the end of the law for righteousness!" "Christ is all." "He must increase" (John 3:30)." I can do all things through Christ" (Phil. 4:13). The love of Christ constrained him. This was Paul's devotion.

IV. Paul's description (vv. 5-7).

"Moses describeth the righteousness which is of the law." Paul used the Old Testament to explain and illustrate the new. See Romans 3:20.

V. Paul's declaration (v. 8).

Oh, the simplicity of it! The Word is nigh. As close as mouth and heart. Just confess and believe (vv. 9-10).

VI. Paul's dogmatism (vv. 11-13).

"Whosoever"—a wonderful word he got from Christ. What grace, what love, what mercy. Of this he was "not ashamed" (v. 11; Rom. 1:16). "Whosoever" leads to the "no difference" of verse 12. "Whosoever shall call" (v. 13). How anxious Christ is to save us!

VII. Paul's distress (v. 14).

"How shall they hear without a preacher?" Sinners must hear to believe. We sing, "I love to tell the story," but do we tell it?

VIII. Paul's determination (vv. 15-21).

His burden was obvious. He shared the desire of God for souls. No substitute for compassion.

A matter of the *voice*—preach (v. 15).
A matter of the *feet*—how beautiful these (v. 15).
A matter of the *heart*—"glad tidings of good things" (v. 15).
A matter of *obedience* (v. 21). Israel was disobedient, sinners are, backsliders are. We dare not be. "To obey is better than sacrifice" (I Sam. 15:22). The great commission is a command!

The Favorite Outline of
HUGH PYLE, Evangelist
Panama City, Florida

FOCUS ON FAILURE IN OUR CHURCHES TODAY

Luke 6:6-10

Why did people attend the synagogue in Jesus' day? Suggested reasons: custom, curiosity, criticism, and for contact with God. This is also true for people today with regard to church attendance. Here in Luke 6:6-10 is a man who did come into contact with the living God.

I. **He was a man with a need that was major: a withered hand (v. 6).** The hand is the symbol of service (Eccles. 9:10). In our churches, there are people with "withered" hands.
   A. There are those who have hands that cannot work in the service of the Master.
   B. There are those who have hands that cannot pray.
   C. There are those who have hands that cannot praise.
   D. There are those who have hands that cannot give.
   E. There are those who have hands that cannot clasp another's in the warmth of fellowship.

II. **He was a man with a need that was manifested: "Rise up, and stand forth in the midst" (v. 8).**
   A. He could have responded with indifference.
   B. He could have responded with fear.
   C. He could have responded with unbelief.
   D. He could have responded with resentment.
   E. He did respond with the obedience of faith.
      1. The obedience of faith involves receiving Christ's Word as authoritative.

      2. The obedience of faith pays no attention to outward circumstances.

III. He was a man with a need that was met.
    A. This man's need was met by Christ's command, "Stretch forth thy hand" (v. 10).
    B. This man's need was met by Christ's power: "his hand was restored whole as the other" (v. 10).

> My Saviour's call I hear,
> "Stand forth, that I may bless;
> Thy withered hand, thy lack of power,
> Thy every need confess."
>
> Confessing all my need,
> Before Thee now I stand
> And hear Thy voice ring strong and clear,
> "Stretch forth thy withered hand."
>
> Bertha Fennell

In our obedience to Christ's commands, tragic failure will be turned into triumphant success.

The Favorite Outline of
T. S. RENDALL, Vice President
Prairie Bible Institute
Three Hills, Alberta, Canada

THE MOUNTAIN OF GOD

Exodus 3

"Now Moses kept the flock of Jethro his father in law, the priest of Midian: and he led the flock to the backside of the desert, and came to the mountain of God, even to Horeb" (Exod. 3:1).

In the life of every Christian, there should be a place of meeting with God. There should be a "burning bush" experience that gives direction to one's life. Moses is an example of one who can be used regardless of his past experiences or present circumstances. The mountain of God was a blessed place for Moses.

I. **The place of contact (Exod. 3:1-2).**
   A. While keeping the flock (v. 1).
   B. On the backside of the desert (v. 1).
   C. Through the angel of the Lord (v. 2).
   D. In a flame of fire (v. 2).

II. **The place of calling (Exod. 3:3-4).**
   A. The action of Moses (v. 3).
   B. The Almighty God (v. 4).
   C. The answer of Moses (v. 4).

III. **The place of consecration (Exod. 3:5-6).**
   A. It is hallowed ground (v. 5).
   B. It is in the presence of God (v. 6).

IV. **The place of concern (Exod. 3:7-9).**
   A. Concern because of affliction (v. 7a).

B. Concern because of sorrow (v. 7b).
C. Concern because of oppression (v. 9).

V. The place of commission (Exod. 3:10-22).
A. The plan of God (vv. 10, 15-22).
B. The plea of Moses (vv. 11, 13).
C. The promise of God (vv. 12, 14).

God had a task to be done, and he chose a man who was busy to do it. Have you come to the mountain of God in your life?

The Favorite Outline of
CLIFF ROBINSON
Chattanooga, Tennessee

A HONEY BEE CHRISTIAN

We are living in a bitter world. The first theme song the Lord ever gave me during my difficult days in Baylor was, "Keep in touch with Jesus, He will keep you sweet."

Jesus said in John, chapter 3:7, "Ye must *be* born again." Nicodemus wanted the honey of God's miracles, and Jesus said, "Ye must *be*."

The bee is a wonderful part of God's creation. A bee has some particular characteristics:

   I. He makes a beeline.

  II. He is always looking for something sweet.

 III. He cooperates with other bees and brings his sweetness back to the beehive.

 IV. He works under the supervision of his leader.

  V. He feeds on what he makes.

 VI. He never runs with dirt dobbers. We are to have no fellowship with the unfruitful works of darkness.

 VII. When he stings, he dies, but at least he is willing to give his life to protect his product.

VIII. He flies a great distance to gather enough nectar to make one teaspoon full of honey.

Remember, you have got to *be* born again to work in God's beehive.

The Favorite Outline of
LESTER ROLOFF, Evangelist
Corpus Christi, Texas

FIVE SOLEMN FACTS

There are five solemn facts with which I want to deal, facts of such vital importance that to ignore them is to willfully reject the warning of God's infallible Word, and deliberately disregard the danger signals of divine truth. Therefore, beware! Eternal issues are at stake.

I. All will not be saved.
Some will be saved, others lost. Make no mistake, let no one deceive you. A day of separation is surely coming, a separation of the wheat from the tares, the good from the bad, the sheep from the goats. (See Matt. 13:30, 41-43, 49-50; 25:31-35, 41, 46.)

II. The majority will be lost.
The majority were lost at the time of the flood—only eight were saved.

The majority were lost in the cities of Sodom and Gomorrah—only three were saved.

Today, the broad way is thronged while the narrow way is trodden by but few (Matt. 7:13-14). It is estimated that only 2 percent of all the people living today are saved; the rest are lost.

III. Many who expect to be saved will perish.
This is the saddest fact of all. Multitudes who confidently expect to be in heaven will awaken when it is too late, to find that they have never been born again.

Then, alas, the bitter cry will be, "Too late, too late!" Jesus warned concerning this in Matthew 7:21-23.

IV. There is no salvation after death.

We read in God's Word of a great gulf which is fixed and impassable (Luke 16:26). This means there is no second chance. If you die unsaved, you will remain unsaved for eternity (Rev. 22:11).

V. This may be your last opportunity to be saved.

God's time for salvation is *now:* "Behold, now is the accepted time; behold, now is the day of salvation" (II Cor. 6:2). This may be your last opportunity because:

A. Life is uncertain (Prov. 27:1; James 4:14).
B. Jesus is coming (Matt. 24:44).
C. The Spirit may cease to strive (Gen. 6:3; Rom. 1:24, 26, 28).

Oh, that you would heed the warning, and right now, before it is forever too late, receive Jesus Christ as your own personal Savior. Will you do it? Do it and do it now!

> *The Favorite Outline of*
> OSWALD J. SMITH, Pastor Emeritus
> The Peoples Church
> Toronto, Ontario, Canada

FIVE MEN AND FIVE TREES

I. **The sinning man behind a tree: the prevailing need for salvation.**

"And they heard the voice of the Lord God walking in the garden in the cool of the day: and Adam and his wife hid themselves from the presence of the Lord God amongst the trees of the garden" (Gen. 3:8).

II. **The seeking man up a tree: the pursuit of salvation.**

"And Jesus entered and passed through Jericho. And, behold, there was a man named Zacchaeus, which was the chief among the publicans, and he was rich. And he sought to see Jesus who he was; and could not for the press, because he was little of stature. And he ran before, and climbed up into a sycamore tree to see him; for he was to pass that way" (Luke 19:1-4).

III. **The sincere man under a tree: the prospect for salvation.**

"Nathanael saith unto him, Whence knowest thou me? Jesus answered and said unto him, Before that Philip called thee, when thou wast under the fig tree, I saw thee" (John 1:48).

IV. **The saved man like a tree: the product of salvation.**

"And he shall be like a tree planted by the rivers of water, that bringeth forth his fruit in his season; his leaf also shall not wither; and whatsoever he doeth shall prosper" (Ps. 1:3).

V. **The sinless man on a tree: the price of salvation.**

"Who his own self bare our sins in his own body on the

tree, that we, being dead to sins, should live unto righteousness: by whose stripes ye were healed" (I Peter 2:24).

The Favorite Outline of
LEHMAN STRAUSS
Philadelphia, Pennsylvania

HEAVEN: "HOME, SWEET HOME" OF GOD'S CHILDREN

Colossians 1:3-6

The Bible doesn't reveal much about heaven. We are told more of what *won't* be there than of what will: the "no mores" of Revelation 21. God apparently didn't intend for us to know too much (II Cor. 12:2-4). What God has revealed belongs "unto us and to our children for ever" (Deut. 29:29).

I. **Heaven is a real and permanent home.**
    A. Heaven is a place (John 14:1-3).
    B. Heaven is a perfect place.

II. **Heaven is a haven of rest (Heb. 4:9).**
    A. Rest from sin (Rev. 21:27).
    B. Rest from labors (Rev. 14:13).
    C. Rest from sorrow (Rev. 21:4).
    D. Rest from pain, physical affliction (Rev. 21:4).

III. **Heaven is a burst of praise.**
    A. Praise is a manifestation of joy.
    B. Sample of the praise and joy of heaven (Rev. 5:11-12).

IV. **Heaven is a habitation with God.**
    A. The sinner will be with his Savior forever (Rev. 21:3).
    B. This is the greatest thing about heaven.

V. **Heaven is a holy completion of knowledge (I Cor. (13:12).**
    A. This answers the question, "Will we know each other in heaven?"

B. We will know why clouds instead of sunshine were over many of our cherished plans, projects, and programs.

VI. Heaven is a happy reunion, a joyous homecoming.

VII. Heaven is a heartbeat away.
A. We often think of heaven as "Far, Far Away," or "Beautiful Isle of Somewhere." Not so! It is just one step away.
B. Paul expressed this thought in Philippians 1:21, 23-24.
C. We will be absent from the body, present with the Lord (II Cor. 5:1, 5).

VIII. Heaven is a hope secured in Christ (Col. 1:5).
A. Heaven is a hope centered in the "truth of the gospel."
B. This is the only hope *any* can have for heaven.
C. How clear the Word of God is about the one way to heaven (John 14:6; see also Acts 4:12).

Are *you* going to heaven? Are you *sure?* You can *know* (John 3:16; I John 5:13).

> *The Favorite Outline of*
> ROBERT L. SUMNER, Director
> Biblical Evangelism
> Brownsburg, Indiana

THE CURE FOR HEART TROUBLE

Jeremiah 17:1-18

Heart trouble is one of America's great medical problems today. Jeremiah tells us that spiritual heart trouble is universal. He gives the nature of the problem and then tells of the cure.

   I. **The indelibility of sin (Jer. 17:1).**
      A. *Engraved* with a pen of iron.
      B. *Embedded* with a point of a diamond.
      C. *Endorsed* by a sinful nature.

  II. **The inability of flesh (Jer. 17:5).**
      A. Trust in the flesh is a *curse*.
      B. Faith in man is false *confidence*.
      C. Departure from the Lord is *condemnation*.

 III. **The incredibility of the heart (Jer. 17:9-10).**
      A. The heart is *deceitful*.
      B. The heart is *desperate*.
      C. God is the *discoverer* of man's heart.
      D. God repays the *doings* of man's heart.

  IV. **The importance of God's cure (Jer. 17:14).**
      A. The great Physician can heal completely.
      B. The gracious Savior can save securely.
      C. The Prince of Peace can calm completely.

You need not continue suffering with spiritual heart disease. Jesus says, "Behold, I stand at the door [of the heart], and knock: if any man hear my voice, and open the door, I will come in to him" (Rev. 3:20).

Will you let Him in now?

The Favorite Outline of
PAUL TASSELL, Pastor
Grandview Park Baptist Church
Des Moines, Iowa

HOW TO MAKE YOUR PLACE THE ONLY PLACE ANYWHERE NEAR YOUR PLACE LIKE YOUR PLACE

"And when they had prayed, the place was shaken where they were assembled together" (Acts 4:31a).

A sign on the porch of a country store read, "There is no place anywhere near this place like this place, so this must be the place." We should all feel this way about our place in God's work. If we are to feel like that about our place it must be:

I. A place of purpose.
A. To help people be saved—this must always have priority (Rom. 10:1).
B. To help people become separated from the world and joined with God (Rom. 12:2; II Cor. 6:14).
C. To help people become soul winners (Prov. 11:30).

II. A place of prayer.
A. Praying and commandments (John 15:7; I John 3:22).
B. Praying and confidence (I John 5:14).
C. Praying and consistency (Luke 11:8).

III. A place of preaching.
A. Preaching that condemns sin.
B. Preaching that converts sinners.
C. Preaching that cleanses saints.
D. Preaching that comforts souls.
E. Preaching that challenges servants.

IV. A place of power (Acts 1:8).
A. Power to overcome sin and worldliness.

B. Power to overcome self and weakness.

C. Power to overcome sorrow and worry.

V. A place of praise (Acts 2:47).

A. God's people are happy people—thank God for the blessings (Ps. 107:8).

B. God's people are helpful people—thank God for the opportunities.

C. God's people are hopeful people—thank God for the Second Coming of the Lord.

Paul had learned in whatsoever state he was in to be content. We can overcome and have victory and success in our place.

The Favorite Outline of
TOM WALLACE, Pastor
Beth Haven Baptist Church
Louisville, Kentucky

REGENERATION

John 3:1-7

Some feel that regeneration is not for everyone, just for a few unfortunates. (Remember, Nicodemus was not an unfortunate.) See God's opinion of man's best (Gen. 6:5, Rom. 3; 7).

I. The meaning of regeneration.
   A. Webster—to cause to be spiritually reborn.
   B. Fairbairn—the change of state and character; a second state of existence.
   C. Cruden—the change and renovation of the soul by the Spirit.
   D. Young—a new creation.
   E. W. E. Vine takes a look at the Greek word for regeneration, *Palingenesia. Palin* means "again" and *genesia* means "birth." Together—"again birth" or "born again."

II. The understanding of regeneration.
   A. Negative: It is not just for drunks or dope addicts; it is not human effort at its best; it is not reformation, confirmation, baptism, or church membership.
   B. Positive: Regeneration is totally of God. Man is the recipient, not the instigator.
   C. The word *regeneration* appears twice in the Bible: once in a cosmical sense, once in a spiritual sense.
      1. The cosmical regeneration: "When the Son of man shall sit in the throne of his glory" (Matt. 19:28). See the condition of the earth after this

regeneration (Isa. 2:4; 11:6; 33:24; 35:5; Luke 1:31-33; Rom. 8:19-23).

2. The spiritual regeneration: A direct act of God by which we are born again or regenerated (Titus 3:5; see also John 3:1-7; I Cor. 2:14).

III. The application of regeneration.

A. There are three powers necessary to produce regeneration:
1. The Man of God (Rom. 10:13-15).
2. The Word of God (James 1:18; I Peter 1:23).
3. The Spirit of God (John 3:6; Titus 3:5).

IV. The effects of regeneration.

Just as in the physical world, God starts with nothing. The evolutionist starts with a nebular mass, primal cell, or a blob of protoplasm. But God creates—the word is *bara,* meaning "from nothing."

A. We become children of God (Rom. 8:16).
B. We become heirs of God (Rom. 8:17).
C. We become joint-heirs with Christ (Rom. 8:17).
D. We have Christ living within (Gal. 2:20).
E. We have the Holy Spirit living within (I Cor. 6:19).

The Favorite Outline of
BOB WARE, Pastor
Tabernacle Baptist Church
Orlando, Florida

A KNOW-SO SALVATION

I John 5:10-13

God's Word clearly teaches the assurance of salvation. The words *know* and *knoweth* appear thirty-three times in the Epistle of I John.

I. **Five reasons why many don't know they are saved.**
   A. Some are seeking through works.
      1. Works do not save (Eph. 2:8-9).
      2. The law does not save (Rom. 3:20).
   B. Others have substituted.
      1. Baptism, church membership, rituals, and reform do not save (Acts 4:12).
      2. Only the new birth saves (John 3:3).
   C. Many ignore the sin question.
      1. All are born sinners (Rom. 3:23).
      2. Repentance must replace pride and self-righteousness (Luke 13:3).
   D. Still others lack faith in God's Word:
      1. They lean on feelings and conduct (Titus 3:5-6).
      2. They lean on experiences instead of Christ (Rom. 10:13).
   E. A number believe assurance is not to be had now.
      1. Believers already have eternal life (John 5:24).
      2. Paul taught it clearly (II Tim. 1:12).

II. **Five ways all can know they are saved.**
   A. The witness of the Spirit.
      1. You'll sense the Spirit within (I John 5:10).
      2. The Spirit of God assures (Rom. 8:16).

B. The Word of God.
   1. Obey and know it (John 1:12; 3:16; 3:36; 5:24; Rom. 10:13).
   2. Written so you can know (I John 5:13).
C. A love toward the brethren.
   1. Who do you really love? (I John 3:14).
   2. Test your fellowship (I John 4:7-8).
D. A desire to obey God's commandments.
   1. Look for that desire within (I John 2:3-5).
   2. Proof of sonship is obedience (John 14:23).
E. Transformation of life and desires.
   1. New life replaces the old (II Cor. 5:17).
   2. The result is pardon (Isa. 55:7); peace (Rom. 5:1); power (I Cor. 10:13).

God's *promise* + Your *faith* + Christ's *work* = *a know-so salvation*

The Favorite Outline of
HAL WEBB, Evangelist
Ridley Park, Pennsylvania

AS HE—SO WE

"As my Father hath sent me, even so send I you." Statement of Jesus (John 20:21). "As he [Jesus] is, so are we in this world." Statement of the apostle John (I John 4:17).

These words recorded by John in his Gospel were spoken by Jesus to His disciples after His resurrection from the dead, prior to His ascension back into heaven. John's statement in his First Epistle refers primarily to our sanctification; Jesus' statement refers primarily to our service in this world. We shall consider the significance of John's words "As he . . . so we." These words identify our close relationship to our Savior in the matter of our Christian service.

I. **We are under a like mandate.** "As my father hath *sent me,* even so *send I you.*"

One dictionary defines *mandate* as "an authoritative command; especially a formal order from a superior court; an authorization to act; an order or commission." A thing that is mandatory is defined as "containing or constituting a command: obligatory."

A. Jesus was sent into this world under the authority and command of His heavenly Father; we as Christians are sent into the world under the authority and command of Jesus. "As he . . . so we."

B. As He obeyed His Father's mandate, so are we obligated to obey His mandate to us. As the Father was sovereign over His Son, so is our Savior sovereign over us. "As he . . . so we."

C. World evangelization is divinely mandatory, the

102

mandate being given by Jesus Christ Himself (Matt. 28:19-20; Mark 16:15; Luke 24:47-48; John 20:21; Acts 1:18).

D. As His entire life on earth was lived in subjection to His Father's divine mandate, so must our lives be spent under His divine mandate to us.

II. We are given a like mantle.

A. Immediately after giving His mandate to them, "He breathed on them, and saith unto them, Receive ye the Holy Ghost" (John 20:22).

B. After telling them that repentance and remission of sins should be preached in His name among all nations, He said, "But tarry ye in the city of Jerusalem, until ye be endued [clothed, mantled, robed] with power from on high" (Luke 24:49).

C. Acts 1:8 is another clear promise of this same mantle of spiritual power from on high.

D. Jesus knew when He placed His mandate upon the Church that it could not be fulfilled with human power, but with the mantle of the same power with which He had been anointed (Luke 4:18; Acts 10:38).

III. We are sent on a like mission.

A. One important part of His mission was to *reveal God to men* (Matt. 11:27; John 1:14-18; 14:9). So must we do (Mark 16:15). "As he . . . so we."

B. He also came to *redeem men to God,* an equally important part of His mission (Luke 1:68, 77-78; 19:10; John 10:16; Gal. 3:13). "As he . . . so we." (Cf. Acts 26:18.)

C. He also came to *build His Church* (Matt. 16:18). "As he . . . so we." (See also Eph. 2:19-22).

IV. We must proclaim a like message.

A. His was a message of God's great love for the world (Luke 15:11-24; John 3:16). "As he . . . so we."

B. His message was also of God's righteousness, holiness, and justice (Matt. 23:13-33). "As he . . . so we."

C. It was a message of forgiveness (Luke 7:36-48; John 8:11). "As he . . . so we."

D. His message was one of repentance and faith (see Mark 1:14-15; 2:17; Luke 13:5; 15:10). "As he . . . so we." (See also Luke 24:46-47; Acts 20:20-21.)

John 20:21-23 constitutes the most important missionary passage in the entire New Testament. Christian, can you say, "As He is in the world, so am I?" Are we faithful as He was faithful?

The Favorite Outline of
G. CHRISTIAN WEISS,
Director of Missions
Back to the Bible Broadcast
Lincoln, Nebraska

THE BEST ROBE

Luke 15:22; Isaiah 61:10

The best robe, according to Isaiah 61:10, is the finished work of Christ. It is more glorious than that worn by elect angels. The righteousness of Christ in contrast to our righteousness (Isa. 64:6) is the best robe because:

  I. **It is free (Isa. 55:1).**

 II. **It is the only robe which can be worn beyond the grave (I Thess. 4:17).**

III. **It is suitable for every occasion (Phil. 3:9).**

IV. **It always fits (Rev. 22:17).**

 V. **It never needs any repairs (John 17:23).**

VI. **It costs so much (I Peter 1:18-19).**

VII. **It can't be taken from you (Rom. 8:35-39).**

The Favorite Outline of
J. OSCAR WELLS, Evangelist
Bethany, Oklahoma

WHAT A DIFFERENCE A DAY MAKES

Proverbs 27:1

What a difference *one* day can make!
The day Pearl Harbor was attacked.
The day the atomic bomb was dropped.
The day the war stopped.

I. The day of sin.
A. Think of the Garden of Eden before sin.
B. Then sin came (Gen. 3:6).
C. The results of sin, even today (Gen. 3:7 ff).

II. The day of suffering.
A. Job had his family and his wealth; he had everything (Job 1:1-3).
B. Then sudden suffering came (Job 1:13-19; 2:7).
C. The response of Job (1:21). We need his faith.

III. The day of salvation.
A. Saul was hating and hunting Christians (Acts 26:9-11).
B. Then salvation came (Acts 26:13-18).
C. The results (Acts 26:19-23).

IV. The day of Spirit-filled living.
A. Before the day of Pentecost the disciples were praying together.
B. Then the Holy Spirit came (Acts 2:1-3).
C. The results—the disciples were miraculously changed and empowered, Peter preached boldly and three thousand were saved (Acts 2:4-47).

106

V. The day of the Savior's coming.

A. Paint a picture of how the world will be before His coming (II Tim. 3:1-13).

B. Then the Savior will come (I Thess. 4:15-17).

C. The results—what a glorious day that will be. All sin gone, all suffering ended, all service over.

What a difference a day makes!

The Favorite Outline of
C. SUMNER WEMP, Vice President
Liberty Baptist College
Lynchburg, Virginia

YOU ARE AN HEIR

I Peter 1:3-5

Today, dear believer friend, *you are an heir* to vast riches. Yours is a wonderful inheritance: it is certain, it is ready now, it is permanent. We are told in our text that Christians have been "begotten . . . to an inheritance." God makes us His children by regeneration at the moment you and I trust Christ as our personal Savior. "And if children, then heirs; heirs of God, and joint-heirs with Christ" (Rom. 8:17). Then the inheritance is ours because we are God's children.

The blood of Christ is the price of our inheritance.
The resurrection of Christ is the proof of our inheritance.
The appearing of Christ shall be the possession of our entire inheritance.

I. The inheritance examined.
A. *Incorruptible*—neither moth, rust, thieves, nor any other destructive force can in any way injure it as they do the earthly inheritance.
B. *Undefiled*—this means untainted, unblemished. In heaven we will have activity without weariness, love without coldness, hope without fear, purity without darkness, songs without sighs, light without shade.
C. *Unfading*—"that fadeth not away." Never withering, disappointing, becoming old and worn. Our inheritance will never be marred.

108

II. The inheritance guaranteed.

The inheritance is safely guarded in heaven—"reserved in heaven for you, who are kept by the power of God through faith unto salvation." The same divine hand that is working on that side of the veil to keep the inheritance for the heirs is at the same time working here to keep the heirs for the inheritance.

A. The Lord goes *before* us (Isa. 52:12).
B. The glory of the Lord is our *rereward* (rear guard) (Isa. 58:8).
C. The Lord is *round about* His people (Ps. 125:2).
D. *Underneath* are the everlasting arms (Deut. 33:27).
E. His banner *over* us is love (Song of Sol. 2:4).

III. The inheritance realized.

"Kept . . . unto salvation ready to be revealed in the last time." The "salvation ready to be revealed" is equivalent to the "inheritance" spoken of in the preceding verse. In Scripture salvation has a three-fold usage:

A. In the *past* experience of every Christian when he trusts Christ as personal Savior—saved from the penalty of sin.
B. In the *present* experience of the Christian, day by day—saved from the control of sin.
C. In the *future* experience of the Christian in the new world, as used in this passage. Salvation then will be experienced in its fullest meaning; complete and eternal deliverance from all the ills that flesh is heir to and all the sins that mar the spirit, and permanent possession of all the perfection and blessedness possible to sinners saved by grace, then clad in glorified bodies.

And this is your inheritance, dear pilgrim friend. It is incorruptible, undefiled, unfading. It brings freedom from want, freedom from fear, freedom from all loneliness and disappointment; it is perfect security, perfect satisfaction, perfect environment, perfect body, perfect mind; it is without any distraction or annoyance, without any pain or trouble, without tears.

The Favorite Outline of
N. A. WOYCHUK, Executive Director
Bible Memory Association International
St. Louis, Missouri

INDEX

Titles of the Favorite Outlines